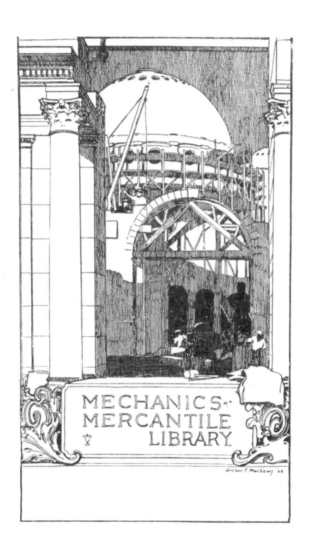

MECHANICS·
MERCANTILE
LIBRARY.

Arthur F. Mathews '06

DOING
MORE
WITH
LESS

The New Way to Wealth

DOING MORE WITH LESS

Bruce Piasecki

WILEY

John Wiley & Sons, Inc.

Published by John Wiley & Sons, Inc., Hoboken, New Jersey.
Published simultaneously in Canada.

Library of Congress Cataloging-in-Publication Data:

Piasecki, Bruce, 1955–
  Doing more with less : the new way to wealth / Bruce W. Piasecki.
    p. cm.
  Includes index.
  ISBN: 978-1-118-17215-5 (hardback)
  ISBN: 978-1-118-22687-2 (ebk)
  ISBN: 978-1-118-23986-5 (ebk)
  ISBN: 978-1-118-24274-2 (ebk)
  1. Thriftiness. 2. Wealth. 3. Competition. 4. Social capital (Sociology). I. Title.
  HG179.P495 2012
  332.024'01—dc23

                                                                2011039736

Printed in the United States of America

10 9 8 7 6 5 4 3 2

Contents

Foreword

...and by it he means the opposite of unity. The case...

Gaining Ground

Do you recall—I mean fully recall—those rare, unplanned, one-on-one conversations you've had from time to time, conversations that took you past all the surface noise in your life, the golf-link banter, the superficial structures of meaning, to a set of ideas that seemed much more true and left you with that "Ah, so this is what it's all about!" feeling?

You are about to start one of those conversations as you begin Bruce Piasecki's *Doing More with Less*—a short book, but not a small one.

Bruce asks you to study the practice of business—or any social undertaking for that matter—at the level of calling. We all instinctively understand the idea of calling and understand that calling asks, "Why are you doing what you're doing?" and "Can I stand foursquare—morally and intellectually—with the choices I make?"

Bruce uses an interesting word, *machine-like*, in this book, and by it he means the opposite of calling. The one is energized, fully committed, imaginative; the other is dull, automatic, deprived of feeling.

The general calling he explores in this book is *frugality*, and as a central idea, it echoes importantly on every page. By the time you close the back cover of this book, it's likely your head will be buzzing as you consider ways in which you can realign your own enterprise in response to the shifting conditions of life that Bruce enumerates. This book cultivates a special sense of social purpose in capitalism, as it refines your particular instincts for innovation and survival.

Look, for example, at Walmart management from Piasecki's point of view. Their executives are responsible for a vast corporate entity, but as the world changed, Walmart didn't have to abandon its core business model or its motto, "Save Money, Live

Better," to become a massive champion of solar power. All they had to do was to realize that their flat store roofs average two acres and that they have almost 8,000 stores globally; by championing solar power, they were doing more with less. Bing! This book explores what Piasecki coins this *art of competitive frugality*.

Here are some of the newly important conditions explored in this book:

- Dynamics between society and business in the near future
- Personal thrift
- Executive authenticity
- Product durability (instead of disposability)
- Market stability in a time of globalization
- Incentives for cultural safety
- Public and business continuity
- Insights into wealth creation and creativity

The book adds, in short order, and with wit and speed, insights into the literature of globalization, product development, change management, and general management, as it provides an original take on the increasing role that sustainability and energy issues play in competitiveness.

This book could not be better timed for our new century. We all know we're at the brink. Bruce Piasecki gives us the framework to look at what's next, without tottering toward failure. We can feel it in our bones that we're poised at the stroke of midnight, and even the current or recent (depending on your perspective) recession feels like an ecological metaphor—that is, like a system out of control and pushed past its limits and natural carrying capacity.

It's in the spirit of these ideas that Bruce poses the challenge to all of us who are connected, in various ways, to the world of enterprise: How do you use your creative and innovative talents in this swift and severe world to free yourself from your self-inhibiting rationalizations, adjust the compass of your professional life, and then bring fresh direction to the endeavors you manage and influence? His vision is a new way to better align money, people, and rules, and his insights are global and of immediate application, as I heard folks say to leaders in government, business, and society at our Gaining Ground summit.

What all of this comes down to, in my view, is the principal responsibility of every business leader and every reader concerned about social trends to cultivate a reliable and favorable view of the future—not the next quarter, but the near and certain future, where our own endeavors prepare a world for our successors.

To his credit and your clear good fortune as a reader, Bruce believes in "the creative power in this return to frugality." That is to say, he believes in *you*—leaders and innovators in business, corporate, and technical spheres—and in your fundamental ability to take stock of change, both short term and tectonic, and make a creative, adaptive, resilient response. He knows this will not be easy, but it is a satisfying transformation before you.

I have more the sensibility of a handwringer than Bruce Piasecki, and I share the serious worries of his colleagues Jared Diamond, Ronald Wright, James Howard Kunstler, Thomas Homer-Dixon, and James Lovelock. In essence these popular observers say that "enough" is neither enough nor soon enough. In reading Bruce Piasecki's work, however, I guess the purpose of his approach and tone is different from those who alert us to impending catastrophe. Piasecki is in the game to change the game. Piasecki writes like a social historian but with the color of a man in action. He is changing the game as he observes its patterns.

Of course, we still need to prepare for something worse than swiftness and severity: namely, many of us know we need to prepare for catastrophe—catastrophe in our financial and corporate and personal institutions. Catastrophe is highly disruptive, and it breaks down systems, as examples such as the earthquake in Haiti and Hurricane Katrina clearly demonstrate to all of us. While aware of the worsening trends, Piasecki sees through all this swiftness and severity and gives you here a set of lasting principles about how we will survive. He is very much about surfing the change to avoid catastrophe.

Of course, a pessimist is just a worried optimist. Along with Bruce Piasecki, I have the hope that our instincts for self-preservation, our desire for social justice, and our appetite for well-being will lead to an era of unprecedented innovation in the marketplace and in community life. Paradoxically, as this book before you dramatically indicates (mostly in the middle chapters), scarcity itself opens new innovative markets. And herein lies the magic that makes this book moving.

Toward the final chapters of this book, Bruce's at times quirky but mesmerizing insights into competition and its complex relationship to frugality grow into an awareness of social diplomacy in a fashion I've never read anywhere else. You cannot say that about many books, except those that last due to their sensibility and humanity.

By the final chapters, on tomorrow and freedom and fate, you will have traveled a long way indeed. By Chapter 4, I felt almost as if I were reading an essay by Ralph Waldo Emerson or another social philosopher of consequence, such as Matthew Arnold. In the process, Piasecki has persuaded and delighted a set of us to become more hopeful, more active.

After all, thrift, apart from its conventional meaning, also can be considered a new road map for the allocation of resources; even saved money has energy and utility. As Bruce notes, "this book offers you a pledge and a promise . . . to find a new creativity in scarcity."

For the past two decades, I have organized the Gaining Ground urban sustainability conferences in the Pacific Northwest. Increasingly, we are a stopover and a sensing platform for some of the best world thinkers on growth and sustainability.

Bruce was a keynote speaker at the second Gaining Ground conference, titled Whole-City Change, back in 2007. He shared the podium with one of the godfathers of sustainability, Paul Hawken; developer extraordinaire John Knott; real estate valuation visionary Scott Muldavin; and Pamela Mang, founding member of Regenesis and creator of the extraordinary city-building process called "story of place." Also at the conference to study North American sustainability thought and practice were more than a dozen of China's top environmental and sustainability leaders (and learn they did from Piasecki and Hawken!).

To this day, I remember Bruce's deft narrative, "Go Green or Go Broke." To appreciate how provocative and trendsetting this was, cast your mind back. Sustainability (if I can lump all modern industrial endeavor and corporate strategy under that common umbrella that Piasecki writes about) has raced from its early-adopter phase to mainstream in the short span of fewer than 10 years.

Back in the 1980s when Bruce began his series of books and his consulting firm, ecological advocates were called tree huggers and radicals. The entire movement was considered woo-woo. It did not understand the role of business in society. Now, the raging debate centers on issues such as the comparative advantages of energy recapture from industrial waste heat versus heat-sourcing from landfills, and the debate is being conducted by folks who wear suits and swap business cards!

There is no missing the longer, truer trend line embodied in Piasecki's work. I first saw it myself in the title of Bruce's prescient talk, back in 2007, when I hired him to speak to my 360 leaders that week. As a result of his particular style and personal force, his *World Inc.* argument has since appeared in Portuguese, Japanese, Italian, Greek, Korean, and other language editions. The world has come around to see the power and opportunity in this line of looking at competition.

In *Doing More with Less*, Piasecki takes his three decades of learning and travel and compels us forward through a mix of narrative nonfiction, personal storytelling, and astute reflections on sports and modern times. This is a book about the management of the relationships between business and society. Moreover, it remains a revolutionary book about how to think about business in our new smaller century.

In eight books now, Piasecki has pointed the way to this smart money view of cultural conflicts. Enterprise has its teeth into sustainability now, as Piasecki predicted. Some see it now as a lion gorging on its recent kill, quieting society. But Piasecki reminds us of a bigger story: this quiet transformation of business positioning is materializing under our feet in a fashion that has changed the lives of 7 billion neighbors. Bruce has been promoting these values and ideas for 30 years, but each new book reapproaches the issues in a more mainstream and more commanding fashion. In the business setting, he has been a green pioneer and a master facilitator. As a consultant to governments and to big business and as a public speaker in many nations and to many smaller firms, he has guided corporate strategic thinking and changed lives. I know many who now see him as the father of social response capitalism, foretold in the next six related chapters.

Here, in *Doing More with Less*, Bruce more deeply and personally unwraps the future for and with you. This master work is transformative stuff. I hope you extract its full and lasting value.

—Gene Miller
Center for Urban Innovation,
Director of the Gaining Ground conferences

Acknowledgments

Emily Dickinson once reminded us that

Earth is short,
And anguish absolute,
And many hurt;
But what of that?

I wrote this book with a feeling of rising social needs always before me, and with an awareness of the years of anguish in trying to make my way, my firm, and my family's wealth in this world. You may say, "But what of that?"

In that brilliant refrain, Emily Dickinson gives us a new equation, some new reason to grow and live into the near future.

I want to acknowledge, first, then, that I wrote this book in search of those kinds of revitalizing reasons and principles. So, I must acknowledge in a primal way the people like my mother, Lillian Anna Piasecki, and my many high school teachers, like Mr. Charles Plummer, who nearly four decades ago gave this poor boy from a factory setting a chance to learn and to grow.

Then I met my wife, Andrea Carol Masters, whose love of fine phrasing and strong argument gave me a reason to learn the power of subtle phrasing and the need to be fair. And then came my loving daughter, Colette, who retaught me all the principles articulated in this short book.

I thank my muse and collegemate Sandy Chizinsky, the owner and founder of Beacon Editing. For 37 years, Ms. Chizinsky has been a passionate reader and responder to my work. She is one of those thoughtful wordsmiths—who can see the value of mercy and kindness over that of cruelty and war. If there is hope in this book about a new golden age, a great deal of the thrust and thought beneath that hope comes from the decades of discussions, thoughtful walks, and meetings with Sandy on the near future.

During the final phase of this book project, I met a most outstanding line editor. As Barbara Kass approached 80 years young this year, she offered me aid and advice on nearly every page of this book, in multiple iterations, with honesty and courage that matched that of Cicero in his best and lasting orations. If faults remain in this text, they are mine, not yours, Barbara. If we had all the time in this world, you would have my prose so consequential, that the cadence of it would be precise and exacting. In your hands, this ideal book would not only change hearts and minds—it would change the world.

But this is a commercial book. I need to thank with some abandon, then, both Kevin Small and Bill Gladstone. They have helped me build bridges to those who make books after the writer has written them. My agent Bill Gladstone, the founder of Waterside Productions, has such a force and freshness right now in his own new books, that I remain astonished at how much time he has had to help me launch this one. Bill noted a few years back, "Bruce, you have been waiting your entire life to write this title."

And Bill was pragmatic enough to find me the astounding team Matt Holt of John Wiley & Sons Inc., brings to a book, from Christine Moore and Lauren Murphy to Susan Moran. They know the force behind personal narrative, and what makes company owners want to write books of consequence.

Books of this nature have become team sports. The Wiley team knows how to win, as does Kevin Small and ResultSource. I feel at home in their settings, ready to run where they request. In a similar vein, I thank my AHC Groupers, Jonathan Ellermann, Ashley Lucas, Marti Simmons, and Ken

Strassner, and Denny Minano and Steve Percy for their attention to the details and the concepts of this book.

As the judgments of history show, writing books that are part personal narrative and part real-world business books takes several different arts folded into one composite style. Many before me have written in this vein, from Marcus Aurelius and Cicero, to Jonathan Edwards and Ralph Waldo Emerson, to George Orwell and E. F. Schumacher. So I cannot end these thanks without acknowledging the many greater books, and greater writers, who have shaped me and my argument with this world. I know who you are, my friends, and you are many.

"Omnes artes, quae ad humanitatem pertinent."

Finally, I thank each of my readers across now eight books, and nearly 18 editions. May you, my readers, become another reason to search, and prove the honey in the tea of my remaining mornings, the warm whisper in an afternoon's whirlwind of obligations one has in running a management-consulting firm, and then when I rest, may I recall all of you with one long final smile.

Competition and the Tangle of Social Needs

A Preamble

*So much for industry, my friends, and attention to one's own business;
but to these we must add frugality, if we would make our industry more
certainly successful.*

—Benjamin Franklin, *The Way to Wealth*

I believe we all have a spirit of competition deep within us. The pleasure we knew when we were kids of doing more with so little is still very much at play in our adult lives. As we learn to compete for attention and results, there is a marvel in our actions and a sense of wonder at being in this world. And that is precisely what this book explores—these primal aspects of being human.

I promise you that this and the following chapters will provide you with information that describes exactly *why* this new century needs something big: the chance to rediscover the vital link between frugality and competition. Rediscovering the pleasures and responsibilities of fair competition is something that adults—those who think they are finished growing—especially need in a time of entitlement and excess. Our globalized world can be a much better place when these adults unite with the new students and emerging leaders. It is a social process to adjust our abilities and tact to these changing and severe times. "Doing more with less" is the set of clustered reorientation points that allows this new growth in society in a time of severe doubt.

Although we all remember how we started, this creative world—and your effectiveness in it—can sometimes feel lost or repressed as we become more professional. The joy of youth decays into the weight of adulthood for many. As we become lawyers or engineers, priests or rabbis, concerned citizens or activists, we fall into patterns of professional discourse and entrenched spirals of peer argumentation. But we can remember our first sense of being competitive in a different way and go back at it again and again, each day. This primal self of invention and frugality allows new growth, even in mature adults. It is a healthy lens through which we can look at this newly globalized world of scarcity and alarm.

Another Way to Wealth

Pat Mahoney, one of the successful chief executive officers (CEOs) quoted in this book, spoke about the pleasures he felt stepping up each rung on the ladder from poverty. "I only regret that my children start too high with too much on the great chain of modern life," he noted at the end of three days of interviews.

Mahoney recently sold over $50 million of his surplus operating equipment and told me the week after the sale, "Now I can start anew with creativity and return to the pleasures of being frugal." He has done this several times in his life. I wondered whether he was being foolish, like King Lear. "Not at all," he said. "I can enter scenes of luxury when I want to lavish rewards on my family and friends, but I do not feel at home there." In other words, he wanted that primal feeling of climbing his way to the top yet again.

Think of this book, then, as a learning tool, a leisurely conversation with the most aspiring side of who you are. You will meet many friends like CEO Pat Mahoney throughout, who will help you unearth competitive advantages on your way to wealth.

Of course, you may be wondering—what exactly do I mean by *wealth?*

In my opinion, wealth includes the full glory of creating and keeping wealth, not just the material gains that come from it. The things that fulfill me are the bonds I have at work and home, balanced with the joys of being a member of a larger society. And this realm of personal growth and social purpose is never static. This book explores the entire role you play in fixing society's many woes—from family and friends, to your firm and the world at large. *That* is your true wealth.

This larger wealth involves social capital, a concept we explore in the middle chapters of this book. It involves taking steps toward the next golden age, a near-future world where the combination of megacities and more purposeful lives form the hub of a globalized community, as explored in the last third of this book. This next global age, I promise you, will be very different—and far luckier—than that projected in the many dread-based books about our near future.

In further enhancing this process, you must embody the principles so staunchly extolled by Benjamin Franklin, and in a sense, become like him—frugal, inventive, and diplomatic. Once you learn to participate in this new, larger form of social wealth creation, the world becomes a more intelligible and acceptable place.

A Faith in Our Future

The magic in frugality is available to many people today. We live in a vast universe of consumer delight, and there are forces that want you to get lost in that vastness. Yet you can choose freedom and magic and less in your life, and this choice will allow you to learn how to better balance the swiftness and severity of modern life.

After extended contemplation, I do not see this set of principles to be about making a Faustian bargain with the near future; instead, I see it as a historic choice of profound common sense. Having known situations where we lose a great deal with the deal, I here endorse an approach that allows men and women to walk in balance. This approach is about returning to a more natural, more native, original sense of balance in our competitive lives, where we know we do not always need to win, and where we know that more is not always the answer.

The social forces noted and celebrated in this book are rising in global significance. These forces will reshape the destiny and life arc of many of you. As a work of social and business history, this book offers a great new age of competitive frugality to each of you—a golden age, in fact, of higher efficiencies, more direct results, and smarter competition. What you'll find within these pages are some early voices articulating this golden near future.

After the last set of business scandals and financial busts, many powerful interests and many influential people are asking questions about doing more with less—from governments and high schools to multinational corporations. They are seeking this realignment as they regain their balance.

A great change is coming, one of historic force. *National Geographic* magazine notes how soon—likely sometime in 2012 or 2013—we will reach our 7 billionth person on Earth. However, they do not note why this will most likely prove a golden age.

It is because our dominant culture misses the creative power in this return to frugality. Many remain distracted by the logic of *more*—in science, in medicine, in mining and technology, and in the electronic toys that litter our floors. Much of what we learned in business about the logic of growth in markets is, frankly, functionally obsolete at this point.

Using this book will prompt you to become part of the answer. You can expect 9 billion people as your neighbors by 2045; you will learn the value of playing hard, not playing hurt in the process. In sum, we explore the rich intricacies that link frugality with competition, and innovation and diplomacy with wealth. Throughout the course of this journey, you will see and understand a better way to use corporate and personal resources.

A Practice in Joy and Satisfaction

But why place this emphasis on money? Why take this thought path as another way to wealth? And why must we have chapters (Chapters 4 and 5 in particular) outlining the importance of managed emotions and the rising significance of compounding value by managing both money and emotions?

The answer is one that we cannot ignore: money makes this world move forward. After much scandal, even money movers, moneymakers, and money lenders are learning now to do more with less. We are all in the same boat at this point, and we share a common global market, with its turbulence and its gifts, as well as the same physical constraints. This set of recurrent universal needs became especially apparent when I looked at the top 60 megacities of this world as part of the initial research deck for this book.

Deep down, humans share a universal set of emotions, which arise from fear and dread of the future, a sense of freedom and fate deeper than national identity or religious affiliation. From Moscow to St. Petersburg, from Stockholm to Edinburgh, from Buenos Aires to São Paolo, each of these great historic cities is ripe for the kinds of innovations in frugality, and for essentially the same historic reasons.

Today's global citizen knows all this instinctively, whether walking up a stairwell in Singapore or Sydney or entering a corporate office in Nairobi, Kenya, or Cordoba, Spain. These awakened citizens have adjusted their lifestyles, from the wonderful walkways of Palermo to the reawakening of efficiencies in Barcelona and Lisbon. They balance their wants and needs, often brilliantly, with style and gusto. I see this gusto for frugality in some of the bright fashion sets coming out of Barcelona and Madrid. There is music and color to their creative frugality.

Overall, in these great cultural centers across the globe, I see a common theme in their celebration of the richness in rules, and in their understanding of what we will call social capital in this book. The people making a difference in our shared near future will cultivate the skills recorded in this book.

But many of us—specifically those in North America, the English-reading world, the old Soviet nexus, and continental Europe—still need to tackle the tangle of social needs, from health care and balanced budgets to lifestyle and work-home issues. We in the wealthier parts of the globe have only begun to see this horizon of opportunities. Many cities and regions do not yet see the promise in the nexus of frugality and innovation. We are, indeed, at an important crossroad.

So much distracts us as a result of our relative wealth—from that dance of debt to the mortgage problems in our neighborhoods to the bald flat tire in our vacation cars. As my wife notes, "The more one has, the more it breaks."

This book offers you a pledge and a promise to outsmart those burdens, and to find a new streamlined creativity in scarcity. In the end, this book is designed to help you look around the corner to the near future, rather than bump and stall like a Hummer trying to park in the tight confines of an ancient urban street.

The Magic of Principles

Rules are often incomprehensible to those who lack principles. Yet in the act of encountering our youth, setbacks in life, and stress at work and at home, we refine a set of existential principles we all share. That is my fundamental discovery in writing this book and traveling this world. In addition, the three global principles explored here are those upon which I founded my firm 30 years ago, so I can fully claim now that they are time-tested.

What are those principles? Let's start with the three basic fuels that organizations run on: money, people, and rules. We all have deep-seated emotions and fundamental prejudices in our attitudes regarding money, people, and rules.

This book offers a fresh approach to competition, and in the process, offers you some liberating new ways to better align these basic fuels in your life, your family, and your firm.

These three elements feed all governments and all corporations. They form the deeper triple bottom line that sustainability advocates articulate and that leads to our near future. Ancient peoples referred to the same human element as "a third eye," seeing a set of lasting truths about money, people, and rules—for it takes human experience, human suffering, and insight to find balance in these competing realms.

One premise of this book is that you matter very much in this realignment. Although we acknowledge that some historic change results from the sheer violence in nature, and some of it resides in the full stupidity of regional differences that change only with great resistance, we speak first in these pages about the kind of manageable progress that remains before you to capture.

The first principle, then, is not to forget the people and the rules in the act of making money. The value of this principle of alignment is clear: when you forget people and rules for long, failure is likely over time. Witness the cases of Enron and its many imitators, as well as all the firms that lose their core talents because they do not operate in a socially acceptable way. The reason we have courts, the press, and vigilance in the investment community is so we can remain, as a culture, hyperfocused on good corporate governance and transparency.

The second principle is a more fundamental one for 2010 to 2050. We need to return to a classic sense of productive restraint, to being agents for the good in this world by doing less. This second humanistic principle helps explain how physical constraints on water, air, and land have affected modern humanity. We must therefore become informed, persuaded, and delighted by encountering our current limits, just as Franklin was slowly persuaded by the powers in the new world.

We must adjust our thoughts to this new world of events. This adjustment theme is not only addressed by priests and ministers, debated in political circles, and considered in public discourse. These topics are discussed everywhere, from the backs of taxis to the YMCA sauna to supermarket aisles. The chapters on scarcity, creativity, freedom, and fate are therefore devoted to helping you consider your best options, given the principal challenges before us from 2010 to 2050.

For example, I predict that our carbon- and capital-constrained new world will have much to learn from the classic writings of the past. When it comes to the nature of fair competition and the need for frugality, ancient classics—from pre-Socratic Greece and Rome to the edge of the modern—are rich with insight. Only in the past 100 to 150 years have large portions of this world forgotten these classics. Our renaissance, then, is to return to being human within a constrained world, where water, air, and land are not taken for granted. These are as precious as breath. They involve an inward errand into the stark wilderness of restraint and teamwork.

The last two industrial centuries have taught us one thing: if you have too much slack, too much excess, you will not be creative. You become less than human. You become the machine. On the other side of totalitarian experiments, if you have too *little* room to move, if you are repressed and depressed, you become the machine also, but from the other direction. We are still, to this day, trying to find the right balance between industrial aggression, you might say, and personal freedom.

I have observed that most successful and happy people learn how best to align their money, people, and rules early in life. They find a creative balance that keeps them in the game with frugality and fun. They are enterprising, not machine-like.

Of course, many still take the dated mechanical thought path. You can see this cultural bias for personal excess and industrial extravagance even in the recent books about Benjamin Franklin (for example, the prized and brilliant historical work by Aspen Institute CEO Walter Isaacson). Although the book is factual and a great read, it modernizes and professionalizes the great Franklin in that it diminishes key elements of his competitive frugality that made him great.

Isaacson popularizes mostly twentieth-century values in his recollections on Franklin. This otherwise great book on Franklin emphasizes his technical wizardry at the expense of his real insight into human nature—namely, that frugality and industriousness are the ways to wealth. This is the original Franklin insight that enabled the modern era, long before oil, airplanes, and our current crises.

This ancient insight into frugality and innovation flies in the face of what our best business schools continue to teach. The principles in this book test and question the basic assumptions of today's dominant consumer culture. Only by accepting this primal creativity in each of us can one find true pleasure and true loyalty. And that is virtually free.

The joy and satisfaction in these principles cannot be easily obtained through any other path. Meditation, being only internal and physiological, does not give it to you. No amount of government regulation or corporate market incentives and rewards will develop the muscles that come from achieving results in this constrained world.

Only you can do that, by going back to the classics on social leadership. In the act of changing the world around you, you will find this world more intelligible. These higher facts about humans engineering their society are deeper than scientific discipline and legal precedent; they involve a need to think through the actions you take as citizen, consumer, and conscious agent in this world. Cultural anthropologists know that emerging and then dominant higher facts come forth from physical changes. This book focuses on what it means to all of us to support 7 billion souls on Earth.

This Is the *You* Century

The last principle, then, is that only *you* can find your competitive advantage for creating wealth. Do not expect your current boss to give it to you, or your parents or grandparents. You cannot get it from any further formal professional schooling.

Business schools are full of cases about teams, and you *do* need to work with teams. But only you can position yourself and your firm for the more severe future and acquire the wisdom it takes to succeed. Everything Franklin wrote, with wit and care, was for you. And you, too, can aspire to that intelligent ideal. Doing more with less is success. Use that as your lifelong mantra. You can meet this century's demands as Franklin met the demands of his century, and you don't need anything except the basic principles laid out in this book.

These principles will help you become adept in the short run and adaptive in the long run. A frugal and fair approach to business prepares you for life and family and allows you to celebrate—rather than exploit—society. Make this book a friend, rather than an order. It will give your life a reason to share.

Our Homage to Benjamin Franklin

This book is my homage to Benjamin Franklin.

As I travel this world, I find that most people know Franklin as a great man, not just a great American. He has become, over 300 years, the first world citizen. He represents to me the wisdom and wit of the past that is ever present. In Chapter 5, which is about the megacities I've visited for work, I reflect on how Franklin's view of capitalism, which is now mine as well, enabled him to live in the new world more satisfactorily than he first had fit in the new America.

Franklin embodies this principle of delighting in doing more with less. By age 41, Franklin believed that he had spent enough time making money; he therefore devoted the second half of his life to making better products and guiding the promising and industrious people whom he felt enhanced society. The people of our new world still admire this approach. Not long ago, in Washington, DC, I met a taxi driver from Qatar, who said: "Ben Franklin—why, he is our man! If he cannot do it, no one can." That athletic chant echoed in my head as I wrote the many drafts of this book, as Franklin's worldliness is more than athletic. It is inspiring to see how Franklin had gotten under that driver's very skin, compelling him to come to Washington to work in the first place.

Nowadays, as I travel in a taxi or a limo to the great cities, a taxi driver will often respond to the name Franklin with this informed joy. I have been testing out this lived experience since my *World Inc.* book took me into eight different foreign editions and multiple countries. These book tours and overseas assignments have taught me a good deal I could not have learned from books. The average foreigner's view of Franklin, for example, is one of a man at the birth of a modern time, one who understood that being industrious and frugal made us *of* this world.

Why is it, in this age of consumerism, that so many in America and the Anglo-European complex now discount that view, and regard as dated the values and art of virtue promoted by Franklin?

The appreciation of Franklin's frugality and worldly diplomacy is not always shared by modern authorities. In fact, as we enter the vast realm of consumer goods, very few can see Franklin's true value to our future.

We should be shocked by Isaacson's excellent new biography because it actually undervalues these points about frugality and intelligent competition in Franklin. What will the new age think of Franklin, if they only learn about his realpolitik, his love of the technical, and his ceaseless horsetrading through Isaacson and other biographers, neglecting the source materials? The Muslim and Asian worlds, for example, appreciate Franklin for what he is, vividly frugal and diplomatic. If you contrast how other countries teach their youth about Franklin from the texts—from India to Indonesia, from Australia to Africa—it's shocking to see how Americans tend to forget that Franklin was the father of frugality, inventiveness, and social diplomacy, not just lightning, science, and dining fraternities in Philadelphia.

Therefore, by paying this restoring homage to Franklin in style and deed, we remind ourselves of that primal first individual who knew about fair competition and frugality when he first walked into Philadelphia more than 300 years ago. In short, we are jiving Franklin's *Autobiography* with the needs of 7 billion new citizens.

This book also examines the works of others who have contributed to the principles described, from E. F. Schumacher to CEOs such as Pat Mahoney. But overall, the main impetus to examine the complex relationships between the arts of competitive frugality and their consequential impact on the world derive from the works and life of Benjamin Franklin.

Franklin is the father of this new approach to wealth, and he is our global citizen to show the way to the next golden age. The following pages are, in the end, based on Franklin's wit, warmth, and good charm. This resonates with many, including a few like Warren Buffett, who are frugal deep down in a Franklin-like fashion. In my experience, confirmed by recent scientific and psychological research, human beings process conflicting information best when they simply learn by doing. We take this approach to refining your understanding of the art of competitive frugality. By suspending our disbelief, revisiting our primal selves, and looking fresh at the great lessons of a respected past, we can grow past our addictions and the illusions of our existing certainties.

Coda

When we consider the current and increasing weight of debt on most industrial and developing nations, we must pause with a sense of deep caution and concern. Governments as we know them are bloated and overextended, except for fewer than 12 of the more than 194 now in existence. We must then consider the twists and turmoil facing most politicians, from Greece to England and the United States, and appreciate how hard it is for them—or for the press that covers them in a kind of frenzy—to focus on anything except the short-term, highly politicized focus of self-interest by which they work. It is very easy to see why they stay within their own narrow areas of control until we all lose control— as evidenced by the cases of the International Monetary Fund (IMF), the World Bank, and our existing overextended mortgage lenders in both Europe and the United States. Finally, when we consider how debt takes the radiance out of so many individuals and companies across the globe today, where the luster of self-determination is lost in the pace of debt, we notice that many of our responses become technical and economical, and we thereby miss the real source of solutions noted in this book.

All experts currently in power must heed the powerful advice given in Franklin's *The Way to Wealth*, or soon be displaced. You'll see his insight goes well beyond the aphorism "a penny saved is a penny earned" and can truly be worth millions, if practiced. This book puts Franklin before all of us as the model of what is achievable to many in this new century.

We have done so many things wrong in reshaping modern industrial cultures over the last 100 to 150 years that a great number of citizens wonder if we can do anything right. In a sense, we *had* to make these mistakes to learn. At this point in my life—and at this turning point in human history—I truly believe that you will make more choices that enjoy results if you put trust in this book's underlying principles and find a path that fulfills.

Doing more with less is success.

★ Opportunity abounds from the realignment of money, people, and rules.

★ By going back to the classics, we can find solutions to waste and excess in society.

★ Think of wealth as an enrichment of life, rather than just moneymaking.

Prelude
Summary

★ Our population will soon reach 7 billion, and doing more with less will be the global mantra.

★ A frugal and fair approach to business prepares you for life.

Competition and the Tangle of Social Needs

Education is what survives after what has been learned has been forgotten.

—B. F. Skinner

1

In the Company
of Knuckleheads

Think for a moment about what you're doing when you run into debt: you give your liberty over to another power. If you cannot pay on time, you are ashamed to see your creditor and fear speaking to him. You might even make poor pitiful sneaking excuses, and as a result, gradually come to lose your veracity. You may even sink into downright lying; for "The second vice is lying, the first is running in debt," as Poor Richard says.
—Benjamin Franklin, *The Way to Wealth*

inadvertently came upon the following insight about competition.

My wife and I were enjoying a National Collegiate Athletic Association (NCAA) final series of college hockey, and had brought our daughter, Colette, then 12, to each game. I will never forget the pleasure of watching my daughter get into the sheer speed and talent of the hockey players' graceful and swift movements. But our bliss was interrupted by four outrageous knuckleheads.

We had up-front box seats as a gift to the last four games, and these four large males were there for each of these instances. As we got into the caliber and skills of the best players from the best teams, all four became louder and more demanding. By the semifinals, they were acting virtually insane, banging their heads and hands against the glass whenever opponents skated by, until they were thrown out by well-dressed security guards.

My daughter asked at intermission, "Are they drunk?"

I had to say no.

She then asked, "Why do they take this so seriously?"

What an insightful question from a mere 12-year-old. Somehow, at this young age, Colette already knew how to resist the influence of the emotionally hijacked. I began to wonder whether adults with high IQs could learn something from my daughter's questions, so I began reapplying everything I had experienced and read using this sports-based understanding of competition.

Franklin encourages us to explore the limits and boundaries to our competitiveness, as he notes how much we tax ourselves with pride, folly, and idleness. This awareness of the self in society is a strong part of Franklin's genius, which contrasts with the knuckleheads' tendency to destroy social value

23

and litter their way to wealth with waste. For it is the sheer opposite of frugality, this knucklehead ability to be so wasteful on matters you cannot fully change.

Before we go much further, I do need to say that I've come to the observations and conclusions in this chapter reluctantly. Our dominant culture, as well as my business and athletic training, taught me to resist this discovery. Nearly everything I learned had taught me to be self-centered in my competitiveness, to help the world by helping myself first.

The notion of social capital—the networks upon which leaders such as Franklin draw to address public needs—stands in sharp contrast to such self-centeredness or team idiocy. Social capital involves shared values that can be exchanged, with enhanced value for many. You see this in games and in companies that value group results more deeply and strongly than those of the individual.

This concept of social capital, which we will explore in Chapters 3 to 6, has a great deal to do with the insights we gain when we compete for frugality and innovation. We'll explore whether social capital embodies a higher set of principles that makes it both different from and richer than emotional intelligence (EI). It is almost as if EI optimizes only the individual—and helps a single person go from good to great—while these ideas of competing for social value or social capital expand the individual into being a citizen and a servant rather than just a competitor. (But more of that in the second half of this book.)

Effective leaders cultivate social capital with care. You see this in those who are chosen as the captains of sports teams, as the chief executive officers (CEOs) and team leaders of corporations, or as the provosts of universities. These leaders have the restraint necessary to leverage the social network to the group's advantage. Yes, every person is entitled to his or her sport, leisure time, and fun. But how many modern men and women bring social value into home and work each hour of each day?

Emily Dickinson was right when she claimed that "the soul selects its own society." But a larger fact looms over this selection process, since we now know through social history how societies select their leaders. Time and again, the filter of selection is based more on social capital than financial capital. This is why billionaires are seldom presidents, and the very wealthy do not run most aspects of this world.

What We Forget in Excess

The truth is that we waste most of our youth in excessive competitiveness, spinning our wheels, and as adults, we need enough excess to spice things up. Perhaps this is why there are so many great quotes about how youth is wasted on the young. This knucklehead devotion to extreme excess is a more serious matter, and it worsens in time because it becomes habitual— almost like an addiction.

Some corporate types are 99 percent self, 1 percent social. They will never be promoted into the future. They feel they *are* the future, however small their actual dungeon and no matter how far afield their best projects. In fact, they call others socialists if they speak about having obligations larger than to their own and their firm's tribe.

In the realms of business and sports, some of this self-centeredness needs to be burnt off as we select and settle our identities. We have a term: bush leagues, where ath-letes are more primal and instinctual, less than their best.

As we mature, some of us enter the bigger leagues. At these higher appointments, managers and executives often tend to have more restraint, more reserve (but not always). As we age, this self-centeredness too often remains, burning our pockets inside out. Some waste effort. Some piss away our shared future.

In this setting of high competition, I built my firm (www.AHCGroup.com) by being aggressive in facilitation and by playing hard. Our lawyers and our researchers, our redeployed executives, and our carefully selected staffers followed with a similar competitiveness. We were called fiercely enterprising. The market rewarded us, guessing we had four times our actual shadow of talents.

But I can now confess that I wasted tremendous amounts of time and energy before I learned, in early midlife, how to be more efficient and frugal, competing with principles as explored by this book.

We now do far more with less: less in terms of wheel-spinning and staff, and more in terms of social consequence. And from this we have received abundant recompense— with less debt and risk, and far more reward in terms of revenue, reputation, and relationships. So I speak from personal discovery when I write about these arts of competitive frugality.

This childish wastefulness is embedded in the way I was trained to compete. I now see, leaving that childishness, where the crux of true leadership resides. We must share in the discovery of the difference between playing hard and playing hurt, between self-aggrandizement and group result—before it is too late. Creative frugality requires this new understanding of effort. Otherwise, we will simply keep winning things that do not matter.

A Gift Available to Youth

Why does it matter *how* we play?

Well, it matters very much because, in the end, our lives gain more value by social capital than by any measure of financial capital.

You can feel and respect reputation far more vividly than the numbers in your foreign accounts. You can avoid tragic falls through succession training and through generosity.

I am not claiming that this alone is the answer to all that lies before us, such as the fierce whims of fate, or the cruelty in harsh circumstance. Instead, I am suggesting there is a wasteful way to deal with the complex balance between freedom and fate. That is the way of the knucklehead. But I am also claiming a stronger idea: you are free to save what you earn, to carve out more freedoms, and to avoid idle wars.

Consider, for example, that the biographies of those who do more with less—who thrive in the face of limits—are far more compelling to most of us than the lives of billionaires. Think here about Joan of Arc or Gandhi or Abraham Lincoln. These were individuals who did so much with so little. They were frugal, endearing social leaders. They stood apart, never allowing the decay of their social capital. This is something we know before college, I suspect.

Playing hard is a matter of good old consistent preparation, training, and good sportsmanship. Playing hurt is cheering in the wrong way, like those knuckleheads at the NCAA series.

I am not referring here to those heroic instances in competitive sports where someone achieves great results while playing physically hurt. I am instead referring to playing hurt in a social and psychological sense—more like a Mike Tyson or a CEO who robs from his own team. These individuals throw restraint to the wind, suspend social need, and cast aside good sportsmanship. Do you see the spectrum of disintegration, or regression into the self, that occurs in such cases? I have read enough case work about the demise of the following large firms that spiraled into bankruptcy to assert a noted parallel between these knucklehead problems (see Figure 1.1).

1. Lehman Brothers
Date of bankruptcy filing: 09/15/08
Assets: $691 billion

7. Chrysler
Date of bankruptcy filing: 04/30/09
Assets: $39 billion

3. WorldCom
Date of bankruptcy filing: 07/21/02
Assets: $103.9 billion

9. Pacific Gas & Electric
Date of bankruptcy filing: 04/06/01
Assets: $36 billion

4. General Motors
Date of bankruptcy filing: 6/1/09
Assets: $91 billion

TEXACO

10. Texaco
Date of bankruptcy filing: 04/12/87
Assets: $34.9 billion

5. Enron
Date of bankruptcy filing: 12/02/01
Assets: $65.5 billion

FIGURE 1.1   Major Firms That Have Filed for Bankruptcy

What we see go wrong in so many sports teams, we see more frequently, and with greater cost, in business.

Playing hurt constitutes the absolute worst long-term way to fulfill your firm's destiny. Most of us now work in firms; the question is whether you perceive it as properly *your* firm. Witness the previously discussed bankruptcies, when firms were staffed and led by unruly knuckleheads. My hunch is that the moment people decide to tax social capital, exploit the welfare of their teams, or ignore their fans or their customers, they enter the realm of the knucklehead.

Achieving Results

So how can we achieve results in a changing world? How can you develop within yourself and your firm and your family the principles of competition that allow you to thrive in this swift and increasingly severe world, a world of global challenge?

To achieve a satisfying solution in our desire to compete in an overpopulated world, we each need to reach for frugality and balance. You need to realign money, people, and rules accordingly. That is the first step back from being just one of the knuckleheads, I believe.

The next chart demonstrates why this urgency for rebalancing is a physical result of population density.

As we add more people to the court, the competition that allows success will and must become more frugal and require greater degrees of innovation. My bet is that this smaller, more populated world, a world advertised in IBM's "smart world" messaging, will require competitors that are team players, at a minimum.

My prior books, *World Inc.* (2007) and *The Surprising Solution* (2010), explored how corporate behavior is changing in a world filled with many billions of people. But neither one paused long enough to explain what truly distorts and disrupts real competition in firms. I've written this chapter—perhaps even this book as a whole—to correct that past simplification of mine.

Why Should We Dig Deeper Than "Good to Great"?

Two things have changed since I wrote those books on globalization and social needs and have therefore inspired this book's broader investigation. First, from 2010 to 2011, several of my clients asked my firm to start benchmarking how companies as great as Toyota and BP "got it wrong" regarding their social risks. BP experienced a more than $20 billion loss in value from its Gulf *Deepwater Horizon* spill, while Toyota had a massive quality mishap that cost it billions and lowered its stock for some time.

This request for more on enterprise risk came from clients at very large firms, including the CEO and chief financial officer (CFO) of Warren Buffett's Shaw Industries, key leaders at Hess, the new chairman at FMC, and a key engineering senior vice president at ConAgra. We also heard rumbling among our 40-plus corporate affiliates. This caused some pause (and some pain) among our staff and our senior associates as well. We realized something in struggling with these questions about anticipating enterprise-wide risks: as a firm, we were hitting all the pistons when it came to the major market-shaping shifts for which we had become known. But we were only beginning to understand what good governance requires when it comes to ranch-betting actions.

Second, I began to answer the requests by giving my clients Jim Collins's recent book, *How the Mighty Fall: And Why Some Companies Never Give In.* This served as a great holiday gift to key clients as my firm approached its thirtieth anniversary in 2011. We all admire the insightful competitiveness of Jim Collins's works. But soon, my clients wanted more. Why? Well, again, the answer was serious shifts in cultural history and significant changes in citizens' expectations. We have experienced several global financial meltdowns since Jim Collins wrote his reflection on the stages of failure.

As Gene Miller notes in the Foreword, many across the world realize these meltdowns come for solid reasons. The person on the street now knows how excessive debt and poor governance can prove, not only in the face of the corporate leaders but also before the people. I have pretty serious discussions on debt relief, reengineering your career, and personal finance with the taxi drivers I encounter as I travel this world. This financial literacy and these debt worries are relatively new this century. They are as mountains each month.

In asking for a chapter like this one, my clients believe that what they need to get to is the very rotten core of this problem in modern competition, not just more insight into corporations. Calling it the "celebration of greed," as we see in such films as the *Wall Street* series starring Michael Douglas, is too simple. My clients and these multinationals need a framework based on a humanistic notion of what "winning means in this new century" (as my Hess client puts it)—a century that has exposed many to risk, not just the elites that run the businesses. And I tend to agree with them. We need to outline a new form of winning that combines lessons from business, life, and everyone's struggle with freedom and fate. Enterprise risk is best governed and managed *not* from the top down. It is not really a technical engineering protocol, nor is it a formal governance challenge, as still suggested by magazines such as *Harvard Business Review* or *Directors and Boards*. Those high-seat views miss the real source of the scandals: the human heart and the lust of leaders. In my estimation, these are issues more in the realm of a Franklin and a Shakespeare than with a Jim Collins or a John Kotter.

The more I began thinking about this, the more I realized knuckleheads have become elemental in business, almost universal in the spectrum of industrial activity after World War II. For example, the cartoon character Dilbert exists as a best seller because we all have our parallel tales of folks at work, folks we meet on the street, and folks in our neighborhoods.

We have evolved a set of rules that allow knuckleheads to walk the halls without transparency, without accountability, hanging their hats on entitlements they have not really earned in life or at work.

What is ailing advanced capitalism is its senility: it has forgotten the ever-vital link between competitiveness and frugality.

In the Company of Knuckleheads

To put this boldly, we have far too many knuckleheads in business today. Some have the calm and confidence of well-paid fools; many are loud and wrong. None are easily realigned to serve society. And although it is easier to spot knuckleheads among sports fans than it is in business (as my 12-year-old daughter adeptly proved), I can assure you after 30 years as a management consultant that they thrive in modern businesses as well.

So who *are* these knuckleheads?

They are the guys and gals who stage highly visible raids during well-attended corporate meetings in support of some highly inconsequential item. They are the opponents of the frugality of effort. They fight for a fleeting kind of attention at headquarters to serve small ends. They simply cannot enjoy a game of serious strategy from afar; after a certain point, they must thrust themselves into a smaller kind of game.

We will unravel this phenomenon in this book slowly. It has crept into our midst, into our headquarters and regional offices, quietly and cleverly over time, like a medieval troubadour who is really a spy in our castle. It needs to be cut out methodically—like the stinging layers in a ripening onion.

The Supernormal Knucklehead

It is normal, of course, to want your team to win. We feel it in our bones, more than we feel the nature of science or law.

We need to cheer as much as we need to smile. But we need to know where fair competition stops and where excessive competitiveness begins.

ESPN reports that every newly built professional sports stadium needs two embedded prison cells in the stadium for knuckleheads. Why is this? These truly unruly fans are becoming a part of the game, both in sport and at work. I even know of corporate headquarters that have resorted to these kinds of panic rooms.

Extreme Sports, Extreme Business Attitudes

The knucklehead is loud and obnoxious. Stadiums train their people to prepare for their frequent and unreasonable behaviors for a reason. Yet overall, the business literature on organizational design (OD) and dynamics and the realms of OD and human resources have gotten fat and weak on all this. They allow such waste to exist.

The key theme here is that many of these corporate and sports knuckleheads are playing hurt. They deserve your help; in a sense, they are crying out for it. Their behavior is based on their underestimation of the value of social capital to their lives. They have lost social perspective. They take risks that hurt themselves and the game itself. I began to wonder if these experiences I had in sports paralleled experiences I was having in business.

From Good to Great to Extreme

What does all this about the entitlements of knuckleheads tell us about competition today? First, it tells me that you cannot fully fix what ails your firm by reading and applying the works of those at Harvard, or even the works of stars such as Jim

Collins and John Kotter. Do not get me wrong; these are great thinkers. But none of them pauses on or knows how to address the knucklehead. When it comes to balancing systems to avoid stupidity, *The Federalist Papers*, from 1787 to 1788, provide a better awareness than all the best business books since.

Our culture continues to allow these hyper people to rise in fame and stature; this is what I mean by playing hurt. It is a more serious problem than those counterproductive elements brilliantly captured in the cartoon series Dilbert. Dilbert only wants us to laugh. But we must find a way to get past this nervous accepting laugh.

Knucklehead thinking is neither good nor great. It is about the excessively competitive self. Knuckleheads no longer question themselves and ask: "Am I interfering with my neighbor's pleasure in the game?" "Is it possible that my family and friends might perceive my actions as questionable?" Instead, some pee in the gas tanks of their opponents' parked cars. When asked why, they report, with a deadpan kind of humor, "Because they have the opposing team's insignia on their back bumper."

In sum, this is a bigger, deeper corporate and social problem than those addressed by Jim Collins in *How the Mighty Fall*, for it involves the *common* man and woman, not just the greats. Collins, the expert observer whose book *Good to Great: Why Some Companies Make the Leap . . . and Others Don't* remains a perennial favorite, outlines in his most recent book the five stages of decline. This assertion sounds about right to me. However, these five stages of decline matter for only about 5 percent of corporate people; specifically, the ones making the key decisions. Jim is exactly insightful for CEOs, CFOs, chief operating officers, and the profit and loss leaders of the business units, and sometimes he is keenly insightful on the aerodynamic drag found in technical executives and general counsel staff.

But here is the bad news.

The vast majority of those populating today's firms are not addressed by Collins's analysis in his great books. When a firm is beginning to descend, well, that's when leaders need to forestall further error and get everyone back to work. Collins now talks of success as luck, because so many of his early cases have been dated fast. He seldom descends from his data-rich celebration of competitiveness to question the knuckleheads in the firm.

Peter Senge and the legendary Peter Drucker differ in their worldviews from the competitive Jim Collins. Drucker was far more like Franklin—witty and aware of human inanity and quite keen on the stupidity of excessive competitiveness. The answer is somewhere between these great minds, back in basic ways of reward and guidance to your staff. Drucker has pursued the difficult thought paths of unlocking the real sources of waste in a firm. Collins focuses at the competitive top, which does not represent more than 3 to 7 percent of most modern firms, in my experience. And the problems are far worse when you get to nonprofits.

I cannot report yet on the rate of knucklehead thinking in the modern corporate mansion. But I have seen boards swayed by similar behavior of chairpersons, except that their knuckleheads did not involve any body parts.

And when I say body parts, I am writing about a paradox in modern life that includes both sexes, in my experience. For example, I work out with women who claim to view life in the firm as more valuable than life in society. You may know many men who have sacrificed common sense and restraint to tip their hats at an Enron-like excess. Perhaps I am being a bit excessive in my rhetoric; however, I do not believe I am stretching too far. Women and men have very often fallen prey to knucklehood since World War II. Our forms of competition have, at times, gone senile when it comes to social purpose.

Whether man or woman, primitive or advanced, the mechanism that allows the mighty to fall involves a switch in one's head that allows for an escalated sense of self-worth and the belief that one can determine the outcome of games that one really does not control. It is as simple as that. If we learn how to use frugality and fair competition to keep that switch off, we have a chance at bringing real value to our lives.

Our Prime Example

You may not have fully visualized yet what I have in mind. Take Craig Coakley, for example, as our prime and most colorful example from sports. He is featured on YouTube and ESPN, and the mainstream press. Trained as a competent plumber, Mr. Coakley is both a frequent buyer of New York Mets home-game tickets—and a knucklehead.

He had a fellow Mets fan paint "Let's Go Mets" on his back. The problem: as he slid into first during the game, he was butt-naked, except for a strange, snake-like kid's toy wrapped around his groin. Thousands took pictures of him, and then millions shared the shot of his backside globally. I see modest parallels in most of the firms I have advised.

He tried to run the bases butt-naked, until he was stopped by one of those stadium security pros who wear FBI-like talking sunglasses. Some fans were going crazy.

In a court deposition, Mr. Coakley stated that his motive "was to help my team." He could not understand why many of his friends felt he'd gone overboard. Nor did he understand why his elderly parents were upset. Nor could he believe that the owners of the Mets blacklisted him. Three times he has been found inside the stadium since his first arrest. He is persistent in a thick way, you might say. I suppose all competitors need a little excess—

thus, cigar parties and other related binges in everyday competitions. Think of the boxers and basketball players who drive fast cars and those who then drive them over cliffs or into walls.

But look at Figure 1.2.

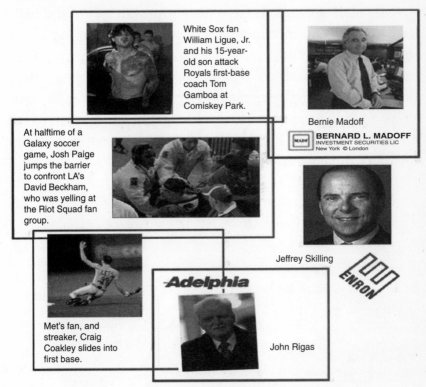

FIGURE 1.2   Knuckleheads in Sports and Business

The behaviors are not unique to sports stars. Some business knuckleheads are violent; others, compulsive. Some white-collar folks are, in fact, criminal, whereas some are simply antisocial. Where do we draw the line? When should good corporate governance and solid organizational training and coaching intervene? And when should the fix reside in social systems? What is your role, as a leader in your firm, in fixing this serious and recurrent set of problems in the modern corporation?

My point is simple, but often overlooked. These imperatives to stop the knuckleheads become more real in a world of increased scarcity.

This has happened before in human societies, from the ancients to the moderns. While it was a trick of Roman rule to try to distract the crowds from harm through sports and massive complexes of entertainment at the Colosseum, it did not work fully in the end. You can cater to the masses for a long time with sports and smoke, and can attempt to appease their needs for increasingly harsher entertainment—but in the end, the game of life requires a greater frugality and a greater kind of restraint. Figure 1.3 displays how reputation in restraint will affect the bottom line.

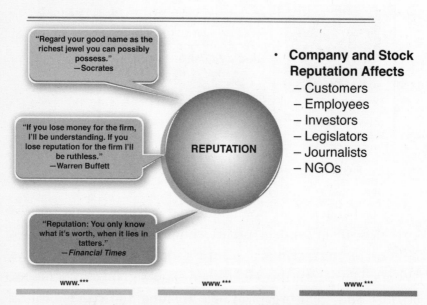

FIGURE 1.3 Managing the Financial Bottom Line Reputation Moved to the Forefront in Valuation
Source: Adopted by AHC Group from Ipsos Public Affairs © 2008.

Frugality—another term for *self-restraint* and *self-control*—is truly the end game of the greats. This need to balance our freedoms and fate takes time; we must build a platform that allows us to develop the skills that people have come to trust. This is a lasting approach to being competitive in the world. The true competitors are trustworthy, even when they lose.

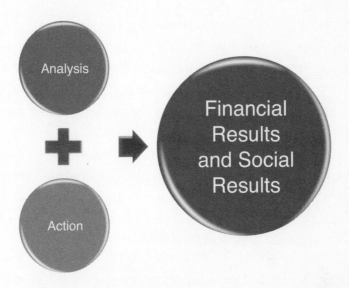

FIGURE 1.4   The Benefits of Competitive Frugality

Our theme is to emphasize the arts and benefits of competitive frugality. The result is fair competition, not just senile competition. The result is mindful. Every competitor must balance preparations, energy, resources, and sense of the situation with actions (see Figure 1.4). Rather than paying the price of knucklehood, you can stand on the shoulders of giants such as Franklin, Lincoln, and Gandhi—thereby bettering your life almost for free. You can travel widely through relatively inexpensive books, as Lincoln did to move from the hinterlands to the White House. You can choose winners by being more selective, rather than by building an immense staff. There *is* another way to wealth.

Walking Home to Wealth

The art of competitive frugality is what sets you free.

However, it is so easy to fall further and further from home if you forget this—and get stuck by repetitive motions. That's why we have rooms full of occupational and professional therapists and the entire caring professions of mental and physical health.

Clinical psychologist James M. Glass sums this up in one telling paragraph that I use to reassert the central kernel of this chapter. We know when someone has wronged society, but it often takes plenty of labels and words to find out *exactly* what is wrong with him or her:

> It is my belief that participatory power cannot be maintained without constant struggle against the tendency to fall back toward delusional or psychotic states in the self, . . . This effect of the self to maintain a psychologically secure reciprocity and mutuality indicates a set of psycho-developmental transitioning from narcissism and omnipotence to consensual reality, or the world of society, law, and historical conceptions of time.

In sum, we are all in the company of knuckleheads. They are abundant in modern society and often descend into the delusional. We must get them to reform their ways. In times of wrong, you cannot find a solution by looking only at the tops of organizations for all the answers. The answers reside in your choices regarding money, people, their rewards, and the very rules that exist at *every* level of your organization. The answer lies in correcting unwarranted excess. You need enough excess in any life, but you do not need excessive excess. I no longer believe the judge of that should be only the self.

Knuckleheads, in retrospect, appear delusional to me. It is just that I tolerated them more, and the time of tolerance is over. We are at midnight in terms of our deliberations. We need to be reschooled in the arts of social leadership through these arts of competitive frugality.

Whether you are a principal in a rural high school, a person developing a new firm on microfinance in Africa or South America, or a relocated middle manager in New Jersey, you have a job before you—so cut the knuckleheads before they cut you.

Leaders we can trust have the power of restraint. They forestall error. Although this is the most frugal and most difficult path, it proves the path to satisfaction and another way to wealth. You may use the principles of this book to develop the ability to leverage social networks, as peer pressure works well against the emerging knucklehead. That will make you competitive in a smaller world.

This takes more than you think.

★ We must burn off our self-centeredness and stop wasting time, energy, and resources.

★ True leaders understand the difference between playing hurt and playing hard. They gain more value in social capital than in any amount of financial capital.

In the Company of Knuckleheads Summary

★ We need to find our competitive advantage through a more frugal path.

★ Knuckleheads disregard the value of building a social network.

★ Truly impactful people such as Franklin, Gandhi, and Lincoln were frugal with time, resources, and friends, which made their ascents possible.

■ ■ ■

For further first reading on this subject, see William Hazlitt's lasting essay "The Prize Fighter." See the latest issues of *ESPN* magazine. Search phrases such as "stupidity in sports."

CHAPTER

2

Scarcity and Creativity

Sloth makes all things difficult, but industry all easy; and, he that riseth late, must trot all day, and shall scarce overtake his business at night; while laziness travels so slowly, that poverty soon overtakes him. Drive thy business, let not that drive thee.

—Benjamin Franklin, *The Way to Wealth*

Often our sense of a buffer—our permission to delay action in our lives—is delusional. The green-eyed girl we wanted in college moves on to a job and a better life. The staffer we had in sight for an important promotion takes another, superior job. The market soon collapses and erodes beneath our best products like our singular footprints in the sand at high tide. We experience the sting of fate and forget that sweeter taste of freedom we felt once in hand.

We know all this by the time we are 10, but spend another decade or two or three learning to forget, as we professionalize our expectations. However, many of us are reminded of what we once knew about competition as we age. And then there are those like Franklin, who never forgot.

What should we make of all this? Why do some get it, keep it, and act on it, while many choose to forget these basics? This chapter explores this process of inquiry.

At first, even with Franklin on our shelves, we think we can hide behind a Stanford diploma, a graduate business degree, an executive Master of Business Administration (MBA) degree, an advanced legal degree in conflict resolution—maybe even celebrate the skills of a high-tech market for a while, or enjoy a cash bubble of real estate deals, as we wait for that more fulfilling job. But then the bubbles burst, and we are left with the first questions of childhood: "What is enough? How do I control my life more rigorously? *What's next?*"

This chapter should serve to remind us of the necessity of investing time wisely from the start, while exploring the inventiveness that we can find beneath scarcity. When someone loses his or her father at the age of three, it is not easy to forget the shortness of time. However, I have found that the disciplines of learning from scarcity require lifelong reminders. So here we ask: What are the finest examples and principles of competitive frugality? How can we share them more rapidly with the next generation that has less to waste? Is there such a thing as life coaching in this area, or must everyone learn on his or her own?

Psychologist B. F. Skinner summed up what we are after quite well when he wrote at the end of his studies, "Education is what survives after what has been learned has been forgotten."

I, for one, am inclined to think that we are already hardwired to consider freedom and fate, even when we are 10. Some learn earlier, perhaps when they watch a grandparent decline and die. It takes some artful competitiveness to create in our own lives a new calculus where we realize we cannot control most things, but rather can advance down a path of creative freedoms with some satisfaction.

The choice remains ours. We simply need to rediscover the force of creativity inherent in our new encounters with scarcity.

A Case in Point

Pat Mahoney, the chief executive officer (CEO) and founder of Energy Answers International, is a frugal client. I had served him for more than 18 years before I learned, in an interview for this book, that he is a devotee of Benjamin Franklin and that "doing more with less" is the enabling mantra of his life.

When we talked at my office, Pat spoke about discovering Franklin's autobiography when he was a young engineer. He described turning the pages with a strange awareness of "what Franklin was going to say next about savings, about frugality. . . . And I knew then what I wanted to do with my work after school."

This CEO is as much about building a frugal worldview as he is about building large and effective machines. I have visited Mahoney in his headquarters, in a restored building on Pearl Street in Albany, New York, for over two decades now, in sun and rain, in winter and summer. And in each case, I observed the same core books by Franklin and others (most notably Ayn Rand and *World Inc.*!) on a shelf behind his head. Sometimes, Pat takes these books off the shelf to read the exact phrasing of a passage he has in mind.

Since reading Franklin's autobiography, Mahoney has built a number of enterprises, including an engineering firm, Smith and Mahoney, and Energy Answers International, a global energy development company. The room is the same, the leader is always alert and clever, but the process of learning how he thinks and works is enriched with time.

A single, billion-dollar project embodies his principles: the Fairfield Renewable Energy Plant. You can find more about Fairfield Renewable Energy at www.EnergyAnswers .com. With the help of federal and state stimulus money, this project will bring 800 new jobs to Baltimore's distressed harbor area.[1] The Fairfield site is near old railroad tracks, and it has boat access from the harbor for barges. This location reduces the need for truck transport, which is one of the things that a local citizens' task force wanted most.

By burning processed waste at the right temperature, residence time, and turbulence, the plant will sell electrical power to the city of Baltimore and the local electric utility. In time, as part of his dream of a renaissance in the harbor area, Pat will sell the excess steam to a tenant paper mill or related industry. The site, once contaminated by military munitions

---

[1] Updates on the project's progress are available at www.EnergyAnswers.com; the Fairfield Renewable Energy Plant can also be tracked through federal and state environmental regulatory agencies.

chemicals, will be transformed from a sacrifice zone into an eco-industrial park.

In short, Pat Mahoney's success has been fueled by the confluence of money, people, and rules.

I was present on October 18, 2010, a key milestone in this project—the date on which the organizers felt they had sufficient approvals and momentum to proceed. Assembled in the large white tent for Fairfield's groundbreaking announcement were Pat Mahoney, CEO, and Pierre Brondeau, the new CEO of FMC (the chemical company that leased the land to Pat's redevelopment firm). Among the more than 185 community leaders were the governor of Maryland and the elegant and articulate mayor of Baltimore.

Since the gathering took place right before the midterm elections, we believed we had a shot at President Obama himself attending. Instead, he sent Bob Perciasepe, the number-two person in the U.S. Environmental Protection Agency. Bob spoke about how right it felt in his heart to find this revitalizing project in Baltimore, the place where he had run the regulatory agency before going to the feds. Even the vice president of human affairs for the U.S. Steelworkers Union was there, asking, in his deep voice, for "my boys" to stand up as a sign of support. Forty union workers, from those who make the boilers for the system to those who would build the plant, got up in silence.

I had first introduced the leaders I work for at FMC to Mahoney's company more than four years earlier. Since that time, Pat has further developed his special skills that prove him trustworthy in complex social settings. The eventual site location and design had a public purpose, and a clear impact that is exceptional: The Fairfield plant will help reduce greenhouse gas emissions from the landfills of Maryland. It will produce energy and steam with a cleaner profile than all of its competing alternatives. And it will bring innovative green jobs to depressed areas of Baltimore.

Some reporters called this a win-win-win project. Although that assessment celebrates its form of competitiveness, it misses the key: Mahoney's projects form a master plan based on insights into frugality and social capital. Mahoney is competitive in a smaller world of industrial excess and resource scarcity.

Well Beyond the Mean

This example points to the lasting differences between playing hard and playing hurt—something every competitor must learn and keep close to his or her scorecard.

If you are hurt, you spend more effort and play inefficiently. But playing hard and creatively is frugal. It is today's equivalent to how Franklin conceived the first public library. You need to balance the efficiencies in self-interest with the long-term social needs. That is Mahoney's exemplary social and industrial genius.

Some people, when they consider the rules and the money flows of this new global economy, assume that you need to be mean and tough. For 10 years, I tried to convince my Rensselaer Polytechnic Institute graduate students that such a silly approach will in time backfire. Meanness proves ineffective, because success is the best measure of social capital.

Mahoney and I have compared notes on this question of moving well beyond the mean. As two rather competitive individuals, we've explored this together over nearly two decades now.

We both find executives should be, as Mahoney phrases it, "cheap, consciously stingy, when voicing their opinions, dislikes, and preferences." Mahoney believes that Franklin taught him how best to involve many different kinds of people and obey the many rules on the way to substantial money. I have found that it pays to align stakeholders without making too much of their differing views. As Mahoney notes, "I find you can do more by saying less most of the time. It is profoundly important to be underestimated in all negotiations." This is yet another distinctive feature of competitive frugality.

Social Capital Is Scarce and Priceless

Mahoney operates well beyond the mean and is a master of the frugal use of social capital. So what do we mean, exactly, by *social capital*—and why does it matter? At times I've described this priceless element as the mutuality in a business deal, but it is actually more complicated than that—and Mahoney shows us why.

Voltaire aptly noted, "The art of medicine consists of amusing the patient while nature cures the disease." This is far more frugal than the modern approach, where excessive insurance allows undue risks, and where excessive interventions by many handlers prevail. No set of doctors can successfully cut away at obesity and hypertension, for example, through expensive surgical techniques. It requires a more frugal behavioral set of changes to repair the patient. Yet letting things play out in proper time is part of the insight from Voltaire, and it is certainly a good insight when it comes to complex business transactions.

My school of management consulting is based on a similar time clock: "The art of good corporate governance consists of healing people and their use of money and rules in a corporate mansion. In these acts you find a competitive frugality that over time cures any disease in business." Some might call this simple; I find it effective. It proves the most frugal form of consulting over time. It helps firms compete for the near future, in which they do or die.

Many of my clients are beginning to note that what ails the modern corporation is its robust ability to do *too much*— too much outside of its core competencies, too much credit, too much debt, too much global Internet, too much intellectual capital with no real future, too much advertising, too much headhunting. These are the things that waste a day and consume a lifetime in business.

In contrast, the successful corporation learns to do more with less, which is the stronger-lasting foundation of success. Nowadays, I find it more profitable to say "No!" 10 times to each "Let's see."

Here is the ugly part. With machines the size of towns and consumers anxious to buy, a large percentage of the modern corporation's mansion is built by people separated from the real decision makers. They are doing a lot that doesn't really matter to the core positioning of the firm. And worse, they are quite isolated, in their high-rise silos, from the market shifts and value shifts in society. They flame out bad ideas without reprimand. As we move to a smaller world, it is important to keep all this waste and disconnection in mind before you start the cure. What I write about frugality is actually revolutionary at heart.

Some economists and politicians think that a discovery of this degree of waste in the modern corporation will pop our economy like an overinflated balloon. These are the folks who say that more lean is too mean. They argue that we need a company's excess, that we need excessive, supply-side economics, in order to grow. I know them to be wrong. The best jobs are in doing less, and the most reliable tax base comes from firms that survive over decades.

A Declaration of Interdependence

If our system remains swift and severe—as I predict it will—over the rest of this century, we will become more interdependent with each month: globalization means regions will align their money, people, and rules in increasingly complex connections. This makes me think back to other turbulent days in human history and ask about the importance of frugality and loyalty in securing a sense of place in a time of want.

Early in the text of the Declaration of Independence, Thomas Jefferson writes of letting "facts be submitted to a candid world." He speaks of pledging "our Lives, our Fortunes and our sacred Honor" to a greater social cause. Money and people tend to be the deciding elements in all human politics; they are often what shape the rules. Each step in Jefferson's work reveals why we must not spend our energy on wasteful anger and bickering but instead invest in the future.

Despite the nuance and abundance in his writing and thinking, the Jeffersonian message was one of immediate value to our budding nation: rules matter. In this way, the Federalists realigned their forces as Mahoney does his stakeholders, but on a larger more emergent scale.

I reread Federalists such as Thomas Jefferson and Benjamin Franklin whenever I tire of all the Washington bickering. Since Reagan and Thatcher, there has been too much mindless wheel spinning in Anglo-American political circles; today's shock jocks and TV experts simply agitate and aggravate to attract numbers, causing some of the stupidity in politics to go global. I predict a more frugal and effective upswing soon.

Jefferson was bold, and wanted us to remain bold and self-sufficient. Yet when you are doing something new and bold, you need loyalty and rock-solid strength to get started.

So what does this mean for competitors today? The rules by which you create value do not reveal enough of the true value beneath the rules. So where is the value (in money and in people) in competing more efficiently within any set of rules?

Rock-Solid Examples

It is easier to see the exceptional in art than in an industrial plant such as Mahoney's. But you can find rock-solid examples of frugality near you every day. My daughter's best teachers are frugal, for example; my knee surgeon is frugal, in stark contrast to some of his colleagues. And my wife is frugal, in that she would rather have one red rose on a key day than a dozen.

In sum, then, frugality exists every day in how leaders spend their time, and in how they allow or disallow the waste of knuckleheads. It is evident in products that survive the tests of time. The things I really treasure I've had for at least three or four decades. My editions of Benjamin Franklin, Michel de Montaigne, Marcus Aurelius, and W. B. Yeats's essays may be frayed from use, but that's what makes them valuable.

I believe the new century wants us to discover the opposite of planned industrial obsolescence. I see this in the phrase "well beyond the mean"—in other words, it celebrates in society anything that is visibly exceptional. Here we mean those things that society comes to favor over time. The phrase might describe an exceptional investor or a key stakeholder in the environmental community. It can refer to a capitalist with a reputation for innovation, such as Steve Jobs or Pat Mahoney. And it can characterize high achievements in a specific field, from industrial chemistry to carpet manufacture. "Well beyond the mean" symbolizes the achievements of social value.

Some refer to this so-called exceptional success as creativity itself, an ability to do something beautiful and valuable with less than your competitors. I find it a dynamic between awareness of scarcity and creative results.

In my experience, if you compete properly over time—and if you are generous in sharing your gifts with friends, staffers, and even competing firms—you amass a great deal of social capital in a short lifetime. Thus, the phrase *well beyond the mean* also implies the ability to create a buffer of sanity—a social cloud around your firm and yourself in this rather turbulent and vicious world.

Visual Examples

To help you visualize this link between being exceptional and being average, we start with an ancient idea—the stone totem. Think now of a stone fetish carved by an expert Zuni craftsperson. It is exceptional. It stands out. You can see and feel these southwestern relics: They are rock-hard. They withstand the wear and tear of being displayed, handled, and shipped across the country to gift shops or carried home in suitcases. They are beautiful, and they are dangerous. The Zuni feel these features near each other in nature and in the human soul. This may prove a lasting insight on how best to survive in our swift and severe world.

Once you visit the dusty origins of these objects in the Zuni lands of New Mexico, you realize that the terrain has been profoundly misnamed: this is actually *old* New Mexico. Some say the Zuni have been carving these stones for 5,000 years.

My point is simple: there is something simple, magical, and compelling about these icons. Think, then, of frugality as making better products, or a better firm, and using less stone in the process. When you do this kind of work, I find the public can trust you, and your staff proves loyal.

These visual examples help me see what is so special and exceptional about Pat Mahoney's industrial ecology approach. He uses fewer of his resources to make power and value for others. Imagine, if you will, how urgent and necessary this combination of social capital and frugality is today, as we pile mountains of waste around the ordinary. The twenty-first century requires that these imperatives be accomplished at once. We have real options.

Finding Loyalty

Once you realign your approach to money and people—and establish proper rules for your own and your organization's approach to competing—you begin to feel a new power in loyalty. Your team then helps you to see the real options that are available to you, and to choose the right projects to create.

I find this process mysterious, curious, and at times, uplifting in that it is unexpected and seldom calculated in your original business plan. But it is worth examining in this chapter on scarcity and creativity. Somehow, in a sense that's both magical and discerning, being loyal to your money and people creates a greater good out of less.

My motto as the captain of several competitive basketball teams was "Once we find loyalty, we have a team." During my first two decades as a management consultant, I updated that mantra to "Finding loyalty is what enables you to last." In either case, you only begin to untangle the future of your firm with trust and loyalty in hand. These social values cannot be abstract, or something you *think* you have. What matters is what *others* think you have. All the rest is simple cash flow management and protection of your contracts.

So it pays to explore this dynamic of finding loyalty. How does Pat Mahoney earn it? And how did I find it? Perhaps the real question is, How will *you* untangle this dynamic as part of your personal and corporate plans?

We start with an empirical observation: There is a relationship between staff selection, your instincts and common sense, and the chance to earn loyalty through frugality. Loyalty turns out to be more profitable and more sustaining than you ever anticipated. It is probably more valuable than compounded interest in most financial institutions today, so it is an item worth mining. Keep cutting out the daily forms of waste in your life and in your firm, and soon the loyalty will shine through like a gemstone.

My experience has proved that my most loyal colleagues are exceptional. That is why you need to select staff with extreme caution and reserve, which comes as a keen result of disciplined thinking. For more than a decade, many of these individuals have stood by, meeting the swift, almost daily changes in assignments beautifully. If you look over their prior corporate histories, you'll find these CEOs, lawyers, and presidents extraordinary, and ready to go after social capital.

Loyalty is an exceptional quality in today's turbulent world. It isn't difficult to see why I failed in my selection of some veterans from J. P. Morgan or why some of my best-trained folks left for Goldman Sachs. Loyalty is as precious as a Zuni stone, but more so; it is a shining gloss on all effort. Loyalty is earned after frugal effort: it comes from others seeing that you have carved social value into your effort.

At this point in life, I see the loyalty in my young staffers. Some echo their parents' values as they talk about finding pleasure in doing more with less; for others, this notion is new. They conserve by taking public transportation instead of the limo or the hundred-dollar taxi. They carry out important results one quiet day after the other, efficiently moving forward, achieving social results.

Achieving results through loyalty is the flip side of pissing away your value by being a knucklehead. You become a magnet for efficient performers this way. I hope you find this importance of loyalty. It takes time, and your example—but it does not cost much.

Losing Ground

I would be lying to you if I said there was this richness of loyalty from the start. There were years of waste, stabbing competitiveness, and wrong hires.

But what I have found is really quite possible for you now. You stop losing ground when you stop spending energy on wasteful gestures, arguments, and competitive fights over price. Instead, you must master your craft like a Zuni stoneworker; you need to outsmart the higher facts of scarcity. For example, I have found it more profitable to explain to first- to five-year hires why I cannot give them something than to just keep piling up their incentive packages. Scarcity is instructive; excess is not.

This is not the same as the traditional recommendation to work hard. Working smart is about not working against yourself or your loyal colleagues. Working smart is about doing more with less. In contrast, we mistakenly believe in modern capitalist settings that we need to be mean and fierce to get ahead. I hear many popular songs and jingles and clichés about the value of meanness.

You know the gruffness I refer to here: From the plane to the train, from the banks to the law offices, we see the damage inflicted by those who lack civility. This hardness lurks in the shadows of most negotiations, which is why Harvard Business School Press has an entire best-selling series on how to deal with difficult people. Although I spent a great deal of time teaching classes in conflict resolution, I now find it better to avoid the conflict—to outsmart the knuckleheads—before the conflict arises. That's smart working.

In sum, most firms that succeed want to attract a frugal set of leaders, a small band of teammates. You can call that team the modern governance and rule-making body in a firm. I add to this that in the end, we—like a Zuni fetish—need to withstand the test of time, across several seasons and markets, and not lose ground in hate and regret. Avoiding the wheel spinning and the knuckleheads in your firm gives you something real in return: you find a more frugal group creativity and loyalty. This gets us much closer to the purposes of money and the essence of smart working. Frugality opens doors to creativity and satisfaction.

My friend and business colleague, Bill Shireman, the founder of the Future 500 leadership network, shares with me a deep belief that making a decision to do something is the first step in making it occur successfully. Bill and I have learned, through experience at many firms, a deep respect for one of Goethe's couplets: "Whatever you can do, or dream you can, begin it! Boldness has genius, power, and magic in it."

The Purpose of Money

Money is not only about currency itself, or the making of more money. Money is about respect, reputation, and revenue; it is about social transactions and social capital. So where did we go wrong? Where did all the knuckleheads come from? Why have vengeance, criminality, extortion, and embezzlement become so common in business? The answer may have something to do with whom you hire, but the underlying reason is in our misplaced sense about money.

Today, if we asked the best trained MBAs from the Institut Européen d'Administration des Affaires (INSEAD) in Paris or from Wharton, Thunderbird, or Harvard, "What do we mean by *money, commerce,* and *company*?" they'd say, "I have no clue. Give me the money." We have, in a sense, gone senile as capitalists. We must combat this cultural senility by realigning the roles of money, people, and rules for our new century.

My friend Mark Strauss, one of Saratoga's legendary Broadway redevelopment minds for the last three decades, feels that he spent a career "battling those forces that make it easy to forget purpose in money." He continues: "For me, it wasn't really a battle. I started from a place of ethics, and worked my way into community, and took my risks with debt and credit with some discipline in mind." Over the last four decades, Saratoga has turned around remarkably, and some of the prime spots are in Mark's considered hands. Mark enjoys talking about loyalty and frugality and the true purposes of money and commerce. "You need to find out what you believe; otherwise, there are too many options," he notes.

Historical accounts show us the real roots of business and money. In ancient Greece and Rome, for example, money came from the goddess of relationships; in Latin, *company* meant those with whom bread was broken. Before the advent of oil and the abstract instruments behind derivatives and high finance, most cultures defined *companies* with a sense of this human and biological scale. In this way, business proved as basic as breath. I believe the frugality of Strauss and Mahoney allows them to see this element as basic as breath in business.

In this context, a company is conceived as a social response to opportunity in a context of real scarcity. You succeed because you are doing something better, with less waste, than your competition. Mark bought his Broadway pieces of the puzzle when they were distressed, and he invested considerable technical and financial resources in his sites. There is a social satisfaction in knowing that *this* is the essence of a good business; success over time resides in a set of rock-hard principles. Mahoney and those Zuni artisans work in the same world—one that is a realm apart from the wasteful. They are not thinking about the next quarter; their quarters mount from the art of competitive frugality.

We end Part I with a further hint: Once you understand your role in addressing the tangle of social needs, you have many options before you and another way to wealth. You have a business full of breath and the future in its bones.

The next parts of this book are about how best to untangle the social needs before you. Part II explores why social history suggests that in the twenty-first century, the urge for greater and more creative frugality will prove unstoppable. Part III then applies this historic insight to a pattern of changes you can and must make within yourself, as tomorrow will tell you this tale with greater force and urgency (offered a source for this book who prefers to remain anonymous).

In the meanwhile, a short finale:

Famed poet W. B. Yeats gets at some of these creative principles in scarcity when he writes about William Blake and the imagination in a wonderful 1897 essay. He notes: "There have been men who loved the future like a mistress, and the future mixed her breath into their breath and shook her hair about them. . . . William Blake was one of those men . . . because in the beginning of important things—in the beginning of love, in the beginning of the day, in the beginning of any work of consequence—there is a moment when we understand more perfectly than we understand again until all is finished."

Yes, you can call that creativity. But in my experience, both as business founder and multinational advisor, you have plenty of options in a world rich with scarcity and social need. This bundle of real world business opportunities requires the disciplined practice of principles, as well as imaginative powers. Social response capitalism awaits your action. Please visit www.WorldIncBook.com for more details, and an extended chapter, on social response capitalism.

⋆ Leaders, such as Pat Mahoney, want to do more with less; they take liberties with creative freedom.

⋆ Money comes as a result of working with different kinds of people and working within the confines of society and its defined rules.

⋆ Working well beyond the mean is having the ability to develop a more creative, better made, beautiful product with less than your competitors, as the Zuni Indians do.

Well Beyond the Mean: Scarcity and Creativity Today Summary

⋆ Loyalty has compounding value that needs to be recognized by leaders who do more with less.

⋆ Companies are created in response to social need when resources are scarce.

Unstoppable Frugality

3

The Art of
Competitive Frugality

*Lost time is never found again; and what we call time enough always
proves little enough: let us then up and be doing, and doing to the purpose.*
—Benjamin Franklin, *The Way to Wealth*

Time is always short, and "anguish absolute, and many hurt," to quote Emily Dickinson. The classics are a valuable source for reminding us to do more with less, since the emphasis is always on the smart doing and the saving of time and effort, without becoming machine-like. For example, Franklin connects diligence with the elimination of distraction, waste, and self-harm. I have argued the same, while adding a comparison to Dilbert in Chapter 1. If our great competitors of tomorrow would keep Franklin in their cubicles, we'd have better products—and a better world. Dilbert would lose, by 2020, his cartoonish material.

Before I wrote this chapter, I reread all my Franklin texts and confirmed that every word of *The Way to Wealth* is relevant to chief executive officers (CEOs) and world leaders today. Franklin is artful, competitive, and clever; he is a master of the business of sportive seriousness. He was far more frugal than we tend to remember, and far more humorous than his legend and actions. He reminds us that the real purpose of money is social, and that we must be inventive to add value as we position for the future.

Franklin embodies a distinctive way of thinking. Franklin's industrial worldview proves right again, for our world and our century. And his principles about intelligently saving and reinvesting in one's seed corn can be applied to today's questions about money, people, and rules; I will show you how.

Money and Rules and the Health of People

The magnificently complex health care legislation passed in March 2010 embodies the compromised but effective ways in which an imperial president works. Today's smaller world requires such realpolitik in both business and society—greater frugality in governments, corporations, and privately held firms, and in the management of your own nest egg. For only frugality guarantees compounded interest.

Through a full-court press, President Obama worked the world media, the Hill, his opponents, and the industry coalitions to get what he (and most of his party) wanted. The net effect: more will have health coverage. But all of us will have key privileges and the significant extras cut from our benefits, like fat from our morning's bacon.

The surprising social and industrial lesson from this change: most of us will learn how to spend less on health care. This was a lesson in which political compromise, complex deal making, and awareness of capital constraints brought all of us into a more frugal way of dealing with our shared future.

The Near Future Is Near

You of course know by now that I call this the art of competitive frugality. But what exactly do I mean by this alluring term? One way to get the definition in practice is by visiting www.allAfrica.com; here, you'll find thousands of cases of women and men putting frustration behind them and discovering that you can deliver milk without the spillage of sachets. As *all Africa* reports: "The outcome of watching so much spilt milk is an injection molded 'Clip It' sachet jug. This is designed to hold a liter sachet of milk securely and at the exact angle needed for mess-free pouring from the source." Every African who is alert to this new frugal device is helping to prevent thousands of gallons of milk from being wasted every year, for very little. The great British economist E. F. Schumacher called these frugal ideas "technologies with a human face." They are more valuable now than ever.

Another area of the world to explore is greater Asia. To get the definition of the art of competitive frugality in practice, go to www.NYTimes.com and put in the word *frugality;* there you'll find examples of productive thrift from India to Indonesia, from Malaysia to the immense continent of Australia. It is easy to see how this theory's principles are global and universal for a variety of social needs.

The following paragraph by a *New York Times* reporter created a stampede of global replies on the creativity in frugality: "Every MBA graduate knows about 'value investing,' but only Indian homemakers apply the principles to peas. That's right: Buy peas in winter, when they are plentiful and cheap. Freeze. Defrost and cook in the summer, when prices spike. . . . Indian companies think like Indian consumers. . . . With all their thrifty proclivities, it was inevitable that Indians would one day make the world's cheapest car. But Tata Motors, based in Mumbai, did not revolutionize the car so much as squeeze $10 savings hundreds of times over."

And there you have it: From frozen peas to new industrial complexes, people make beautiful decisions when they put society above their fears.

Now let's return to the issue at hand: how best to preserve our vital resources for the future.

Rules Regarding the Near Future

Part of the art of competitive frugality means to me that decision makers—from CEOs to the leaders of nations—are finding new ways to do more with less. This is not an academic distinction or discipline but a feature of contemporary social history. They are cherishing their seed corn, not spilling it. This is nearly biblical in its consequence, a return to our primal beliefs about stewardship and purpose in life.

The reason is simple: There are many more of us—7 billion at least—in this smaller world, where we must share our health care, our milk, and our products. And since we all consume more than our grandfathers, there is a sense of urgency to this search for frugality.

In this smaller, twenty-first-century world, we must all become like Benjamin Franklin all over again. Blending frugality and industriousness is more primal than engaging in technology for technology's sake or doing science "because it can be done." We must face the higher facts of scarcity and creativity head-on this century: the age of the consumer is giving way to a more creative age of restraint.

The Path Forward Is Together

Provost William Throop, of Green Mountain College, in Vermont, centers his school on educating for the near future. He notes that as we encounter and successfully outmaneuver limits, "The world becomes more intelligible . . . we feel accomplished and satisfied because to participate in a larger social journey, with a set of smart competitors, makes us grow."

"Humans are hardwired for this kind of competition," Throop continues, "and I've come to believe that the logic of frugality is our path forward together. Over time . . . frugality is the central rallying call that will bring forward both leaders and new potential in the [coming] generation of designers, thinkers, and doers." Throop's reply to my questions define the rich domain of this next chapter. While we started the inquiry on health care in an overpopulated world, we are extending the example to encompass competitive frugality in general.

For example, drawing on this sharp new awareness of limits, even politicians with visions as grand as those of President Obama are exacting compromises on taxes, health care, the military budgets, the number of our wars, and how we spend our excess. Most important, corporations facing real material constraints are learning to compete for more with less.

How These New Rules Constitute Higher Facts

For years, experts measured how the world was muddling toward frugality in terms of gross domestic products, the health of economies, and our rate of consumption. Such studies are usually empirical and based on trends, and they do help frame our debate. But here we write about a set of higher facts that define the world in which we now live—whether rich or poor, industrialized or aspiring to be industrialized. This is the world of the near future. It is swift. It is severe. It is near.

These are the higher rules that enable a fully formed leader to be creative in new constrained situations and downturns. They are also the rules that allow new-century beginners to take leaps forward when they rethink their future. These are the rules about frugality and competitiveness that define our new world of scarcity, where water and land and food and energy are more precious than ever. Let's view this as a positive social result of the last 40 Earth Days.

But do the new rules in this book constitute a set of higher facts—a shift in worldview, you might say? When we consider the decrease in arable land per person since World War II— and the scarcity this implies for energy and industrial production, as well as world needs—you begin to see this artful need.

This is why, in a nutshell, I think it pays to consider the rules of frugality as a set of higher facts. The world has become swift and severe; that is for sure. Most of my clients understand that as they start their days across the cities of this world. This swift and severe world forms a new S Frontier, defined in Figure 3.1—one where most are driven down the S into pressured lives. It is easier, in a way, to spend downward into pressure, until you learn how to conserve to save upward. But some who are frugal, creative, and clever—what we used to call street smart—start to rise on the S Frontier increasingly earlier in this life. I have seen that tendency occur again and again in leadership circles.

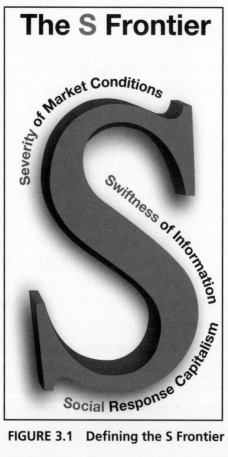

FIGURE 3.1 Defining the S Frontier

My high school teacher, Mr. Plummer, had me reflect this way: "Next time you are on the beach, Bruce, look at the people who learn quickly how to body surf, and watch all the others that get wiped out." Some call this existential dread; I call it my daily soup.

In Chapter 4, we explore these dynamics of freedom and fate more intensively. But for now, we leave it as an image that the world has indeed changed. It has become swifter and more severe, and this alone requires the freedom to choose, which is evident when we are frugal.

Yet for years I did not pause long enough to contemplate the full meaning of this change. There are winners and losers in this globalized capitalist world, where the social safety net is less derived from governments than in the past. You need to be a weaver of that net for yourself, your career, and your family before it begins fraying in your life. The best way to do this is to do more with less—that is, to save a certain percentage of your earnings from the start, to compound value and safety as you move forward.

Here is the more potent fact: we live in an age of social response capitalism, a world where we compete on price, quality, *and* social needs.

Providing your family and yourself with adequate health care coverage is a likely and unfortunate necessity today. It is, in addition, a major expense in running a business, and the expense grows significantly with each new hire. To do this right, you must be ready to conserve. That is where the successful reside. If you accept this fundamental need to set aside reserves as a guiding principle, you will begin to ascend into the new century thinking.

Whether we are facing health risks, floods, or collapsing roofs, car accidents, or other untoward events during work or play, we have the right to ask for help. And society has a job to offer that help. But much depends on our ability to surf the S Frontier. We must recognize what we can control, build some reserves, and then protect what we have attained. Shakespeare has a lovely phrase that made me save: "So shall I taste at first the very worst of fortune's might." In other words, we have the responsibility to anticipate harm before it happens and set aside reserves so that we can manage it.

The Higher Facts of Health Care

Health care reform at the turn of this new century was a known social need around the globe. Nations were betting more and more of their budget on caring for the elderly, the traumatized, and the hurt, without creating adequate reserves. Here in the United States, after the election of President Obama, we could no longer afford doing without health care, but we could not afford its future price at the quality we expected. Thus, let's pay attention to this modern-day and frugal compromise. It is a harbinger of things to come; we should pay attention to it.

Social history is always reactive, a rebalancing of the roles of government, innovations in science and technology, and the logic of markets. President Obama arose from a historic context: his election was the culmination of a three-decade response to the policies of Ronald Reagan and Margaret Thatcher. But the real lesson is to be found in corporate mansions, well outside of the great capitals of the world. Doing more with less is becoming the mantra of General Electric, Walmart, Google, and other global giants that I refer to as World Inc. firms. (Please see abundant free resources on this concept at www.WorldIncBook.com.)

Who Runs the World, If Not Nation-States?

What have I learned from watching the first few years of President Obama's administration? What have I learned from other newly elected leaders, from Turkey to the Latin countries? Not as much as I learned from watching the great corporations over the last 10 years! This physical push for doing more with less is born from corporate discipline and personal choice, more than from any kind of formal government policy.

It is the corporations that have responded to the needs of today. If you look hard at poverty and disease, and the strains on water, land, and forests, you will see that governments and nonprofits frame the questions that corporations rise to answer. This has been the trend in the twenty-first century so far. I find this remarkably different from Roman times, or say from the times when America was getting its footing after the publication of the *Federalist Papers*.

As I explained in my last two books, the last 10 years have essentially forced us to learn the classic art of corporate frugality all over again and apply it aggressively in industrial cultures from Asia to Europe to North America. This new focus has reshaped politics, corporate life, and even our nest eggs in the blink of a few seasons. I see it as the great differentiator in corporate and political life. The forms of poverty that exist today can be answered only by a global surge of artful competitive frugality (see Figure 3.2).

This demand for competitive frugality did not come from national leaders; it is a newly extraordinary feature of advanced industrialism. While the evening news entertains us with talking heads saying little of long-term consequence, the quiet insistent call for frugality rises in its cadences.

Economic poverty:
• Over 2 billion people living on less than $2 a day

Energy poverty:
• 1.6 billion people today without access to electricity

Mobility poverty:
• 900 million people without access to transportation

Water poverty:
• 1.8 million deaths per year due to lack of sanitation, poor hygiene, and unsafe drinking water

FIGURE 3.2   The Poverty of Today

Why does this matter? Well, if we fail to adjust to this higher imperative for competing on frugality, we will feel the severity of limits even more strongly. If we do not make the necessary shifts in attitude and values (in response to the facts listed in Figure 3.2), the fabulous complexities of money will continue to baffle and hurt us. We will be propelled down the S Frontier, rather than enriched by it.

Many Europeans and Americans mistakenly believe that when it comes to complex issues—from fossil fuels to immigration to health care—we can bring about the necessary changes through regulation alone. Since World War II, many nations act as if rule making trumped the shaping of money, and investments, and the direction of people.

But, in a carbon and capital-constrained world, regulation is not enough. Regulation alone provides less than half the pair of scissors needed to cut through the wordly problems.

The corporations—at least the best ones—understand this. They reinvest in their people and reshape their spending as they continuously realign to social changes and market forces. Sure, rules are part of the grand mix that allows the flow of money and the rise or fall of people. History shows us that rules define the average, the floor, the base, and the mean. But to think rules are the only answer is to resist something fundamental in human nature. We'd rather find a fair and competitive answer to a problem than be told what to do. We want to race up the stairwell of the S Frontier.

Here is what I see in today's world: We must go global as we go green. We must go lean, as this world is far swifter than our best thoughts. It will punish the wasteful and waste the wrong-headed knuckleheads over time.

Money and people will reshape these issues more rapidly than the most ambitious set of new rules established by governors or other elected officials. Rules, in my experience, simply stabilize new sets of social facts, such as those over car emissions or the ones meant to protect us from drunk or speeding drivers. But if rules are A to C, it is money and people that enrich and complete the alphabet of industrial societies.

Witness the seat belt, the new rules on eliminating wasteful lightbulbs, and the way that the Environmental Protection Agency is regulating CO_2 in the absence of congressional alignment. Early adopters shape possible and needed change, and then money rapidly follows the opportunity in the new, more demanding rules. That is the way of this world. This book's job is to get you from D to Z, not to state the rules you already know need to be enacted.

Another way to sum up this new path to social leadership is to contemplate this paradox: the corporate world, which is the leading force shaping social history today, is far more competitive than our best philosophies and time-honored beliefs. This might be why so many of our professional schools are decades behind the state of the art in companies.

Miseducation has its consequences: Modern business leaders tend to scoff at risk and celebrate the bold try. The professors of enterprise glorify the risky, and for years they touted the greatness of an Enron, clearly without knowing all the facts. It does not make sense to push on in the old ways when the result could be chaos and certain loss. Yet I've often found that the modern MBA forgets the classic lessons in caution, inventiveness, and frugality. After all, while I was building my firm, I spent 44 semesters teaching—so I believe I've seen the larger pattern here. Until the Enron bubble, the derivatives markets, and the real estate bubbles burst, most faculty left a trail of naïve praise in their publications, as did the business journals and mainstream press.

This is why we need to become like Benjamin Franklin, and, in the coming decades, become incredibly inventive in developing new forms of energy. We must also be incredibly frugal in our investments. As the BP Gulf spill proves, a mistake in a swift world can cost a firm $20 billion. As we learned from watching Toyota respond to public scrutiny of its safety and quality issues, the tolerance for knuckleheads in this new century is at an all-time low. You need to throw away those old business school myths and face the higher facts.

To achieve peace and prosperity—to reach that next golden age—we must develop and disseminate the art of frugality. The next golden age will be about a frugal prosperity for a growing number of people. The well-dressed ambassadors of frugality must offer this logic as the long sword of our politics, as the hymn of our workdays and our nights.

The way to take action is to note the rising relationships between financial demands for frugality, the challenges for efficiency from carbon- and energy-usage patterns, and the loud recurrent calls for sustainability. The masters of business administration need to return to these shaping concerns soon.

If Thought Ran This Zoo

With the foamy tempest of this new century still rolling its salt and spray before us, we need to look ahead with the resolve of a lone fisherman in a storm. Forget the hordes of analysts who loved the Enrons, the Lucents, the big bets. The best in us will bring forth this artful frugality.

I am certain that in a few short years (definitely by my eightieth birthday, in 2035), we will see rapid and contentious legislative changes on big issues such as carbon taxes, renewable energy portfolio requirements, and tax requirements for small and large companies alike.

Social advocates often say there is not enough time, that a gradual move to frugality will cost us far too much in terms of the price of oil, our homes, and our cars. I beg to differ, because I'm seeing this change happening already. The recognition of the need for frugality has been at a low simmer since World War II, but we're likely to see the rules and money realign faster and faster as the population reaches that 7 billionth person.

A Zookeeper's Retrospect

In my youth, right after completing my doctoral work at Cornell, I worked in Washington, DC, on legislative affairs. Back then—during the Carter, Reagan, and first Bush administrations—talking about conservation and frugality was perceived by many to be socialist and anti-American. While I was writing my first two legislation-heavy books in the 1980s—and while I interacted with these legislators—I sensed a significant blindness in the whole political system, a refusal to face real facts.

This blindness—this refusal to ask questions about linking global competitiveness with frugality—granted me some interesting opportunities, which I exploited with speed and aggression. Passage of the Superfund program and the Resource Conservation and Recovery Act brought many strange bedfellows in politics—and in the marketplace—into alignment. Rather rapidly, we shifted from dumping industrial chemicals into pits, ponds, and industrial lagoons to establishing a market for treatment and cleanup.

Here is my point: the entire global political system—from the United Kingdom to the United States to Australia and Africa—is now being overhauled due to acknowledged physical and financial constraints. Are we there yet, you might ask? Of course, the answer is no. But the patterns are quite clear if you look at them from the lens of competition for limited resources.

If thought ran this zoo—instead of prejudice and power— we would have some of these thought paths firmly in place by now. Nation by nation, we would have become aligned with the principles of doing more with less. My point: Do not stop there, since time and again, we know what happens to prejudice and dated power over time.

Upon leaving Washington, I went walking into the future. As I walked, I built a firm known as a change agent. For years, they called us facilitators of social response capitalism. Tomorrow will tell more. The near future is near; this is what I foresee for your next three to four decades.

I can see by 2015 large urban towers, skyscrapers devoted to food production to address the food imbalances for additional people. We'll see these first in Asia, then in the most crowded areas of Europe, and then, before 2045, I believe we'll see them in the fertile crescents of the United States—from the Northeast to the Midwest congressional districts and perhaps in California.

This will occur for the simple reason that we can no longer grow enough food on the traditional two-dimensional farm. We can have an organic revolution in Burlington or Middlebury, Vermont, and in a small town such as the one where I live. But looking over the entire canvas, you can expect only the megafood producers such as ConAgra, Unilever, Coca-Cola, and others to go this multistoried route soon.

I already see rapid progress in renewable energy, as the net production of conventional oil continues to decline annually. I currently sit on the board of Washington's Sustainable Business Alliance, and I see the topic of renewable energy arising at each meeting. I also sit on the advisory board of an Athens-based firm with leaders from India, France, and Japan, and we are looking systematically at renewable resources from Greece and the Balkans to wherever money can flow.

I already see the emergence of smarter products such as hybrid power trains in cars, less toxic metals in computers, and more efficient homes. You can expect Warren Buffett's Burlington Northern Santa Fe (BNSF) and our corporate affiliates, CSX and Canadian National Railway, to make these adjustments relatively soon—and this is only a start. My prior books have been enriched by these early examples, and our corporate affiliate workshops are filled with even more. The principles we explore in this book are generalizations based on fact, outlines of the near future.

What matters now is your arrival to this way of thinking and acting. Around which element of this social race, this untangling of key needs, do you want to center your competitiveness? (See Figure 3.3.) My staff is looking at renewable energy, smart investing, the careful redesign of autos and mobility, the future of rail in a time of carbon, the future of flooring, and the production of food in ways that are less dependent on fossil fuels. And so are our many healthy competitors.

❖ Urbanization	❖ Decreasing Energy Reserves
❖ Aging Populations	❖ Water Scarcity
❖ Climate Change	❖ Scarcity of Arable Land
❖ Globalization	

FIGURE 3.3   Key Megatrends Inspiring Competitive Frugality

You can sense these larger waves mounting if you merely adjust your thinking. What I write about is social history, not just personal narrative.

Here is what we can expect: The next wave after health care reform will produce a stronger, more global set of financial reforms. I predict that by 2020, a mere nine years from now, we will see serious and sustained corporate reform of governing boards and member selection processes.

By 2030, the arts of competitive frugality will be in full force regarding agribusiness. Firms, including Cargill, ConAgra, Smithfield Farms, and beverage giants Diageo and Coca-Cola, are developing very sophisticated business plans based on the principles of sustainability recited in this book. The required skills of managerial accounting will be matched by skills in competitive frugality, for the first time in publicly held organizations.

By 2030, this approach will soon cascade down to all profit and loss leaders at all manufacturing firms, and it will rapidly green even the most reluctant chief financial officers and chief operating officers. A workshop series we run for many large organizations called "Competing on Sustainability" will not only be an intention but will be a competitive advantage. This means that all corporate leaders who soon get the need for sustainability will rise visibly, as the others fail to realize this logic. In the end, global capitalism becomes social response capitalism by 2030. Again, some will ask if we can wait this additional 19 years. Many will fail in the waiting.

This is a swiftly emerging and harsh new truth. Markets will reward those who come first to the idea that there is less land per person to supply needed food and energy. Meeting these challenges will involve rapid important shifts to alternative fuels and will allow what I've called a World Inc. bloodless revolution in products and processes (*World Inc.*, Sourcebooks, 2007).

In short, I predict that a single theme will dominate our next two decades in business and society: we will need to do more with less. From government to large and small firms, as well as families, this will be our calling.

For other examples of frugality in action, punch in:

- www.allAfrica.com/stories
- www.MoneyShow.com/investing
- www.AsiaNewsNet.net/home/news
- www.EthiopianReporter.com/english/index
- www.TheJakartaGlobe.com/opinion
- www.BusinessAndEconomy.org
- In working in corporate and social change management for more than 30 years, I can say with certainty there has never before been so much global interest in doing more with less.

★ Today's smaller world requires frugality from governments, corporations, privately held firms, and individual homes.

★ Limits allow us to find a new frugal approach to a problem such as how we will spend less on health care by responding to the needs of many individuals.

★ The age of the consumer is giving way to a more creative age of restraint.

★ Corporations are discovering ways to address poverty, disease, and strains on water, land, and forests through innovation.

★ The severity of limits will become more evident if we do not make the necessary shift toward innovation and frugality.

The Art
of
Competitive
Frugality
Summary

4

Doing More with Less

An Essay on Freedom and Fate

We are taxed twice as much by our idleness, three times as much by our pride, and four times as much by our folly.
—Benjamin Franklin, *The Way to Wealth*

I have been lucky in life. Born poor, I learned the skills of doing more with less early on. I saw firsthand how close invention and creativity and diplomacy sit near frugality. These choices sat in my head like competing family members.

I learned from my mother to act with the spirit of frugality and to mimic the older sisters of invention and diplomacy. After my father died when I was three years old, my mother, Lillian Anna Piasecki, took in foster children from New York City foundling homes to make ends meet. From Lillian, I learned how painfully accurate Franklin's warnings about folly, pride, and idleness prove to lives with little margin of protection.

I grew up in suburban Long Island without a car or the money to eat out. This scarcity of means actually gave me the time and opportunity to explore my interests and shape my own way. We finished meals rapidly, and the days were long with discovery. Those who are born into a shortage of wealth are not surrounded by activities and obligations or the rules of professional expectations. We start early with direct action and risk taking. And the warring articulate sisters of fate inside our heads are always judging, always evaluating what works and what does not work, as they outline a faint path in the sand for us to follow.

My upbringing granted me a full decade of trial and discovery in the arts of competitive frugality before being surrounded by the so-called advantages of college. You can call this a long foreground. My point is simpler. There was a war going on inside my young mind, where many voices churned, urging that I become a soldier or a priest, an athlete or a professional. These voices were my playbook, and my guidance system was tuned from direct experiences filtered through my mother's principles. I heard her commands in a fashion more restless than logical. In fact, in my way of feeling, these early decisions to go athletic or go military were my Harvard and Yale before Cornell.

My Chinese sister Susie Ying Chang and my Puerto Rican brothers Edwin Torres and Theo taught me how to navigate past the prejudices and knucklehead behaviors we encountered at school and on the street. I learned that some schoolteachers and established well-intentioned professionals were ignorant of what motivated the poor.

They would punish us based on superficial rules, just to save face or cater to their bosses. They would not pause to understand the reasoning behind our actions. These established authorities, from principals to priests, from coaches to select sports fans, would often miss the point of half of my conversation—in short, why I did what I did. Then they would completely overlook that my mistake resulted from a conscious effort to learn by doing. Many of the poor simply give up explaining their thinking and go underground, in a sense. Often I would be called into the principal's office, only to find out that a new teacher did not believe Edwin Torres was my brother.

But there was a larger lesson looming from this period. During my teens, I came to see nearly all people's lives in terms of what they were able to do after (and as a reaction to) resistance or repression or abuse. I would not stay long in any stressful situation because that would allow life's severities to take me down a step or two. I told myself I would not complain to friends about an adult's misunderstanding for more than one day. With little real supervision, I refused to allow personal defeats to fester.

This is what I mean when I say that the world of events is always faster than our thoughts. We all experience the complex mix of reward, punishment, and constant feedback routinely handed out to youth. What adds up in the end is what you choose to do with the world's severity on a daily basis.[1]

Fast-Forward

I experienced a contemporary example of what I refer to as posttraumatic growth while writing this book. Last year I heard Susan Retik, president and cofounder of an organization called Beyond the 11th, speak at Skidmore College. She spoke with animation and conviction, and I was moved, as were my wife, mother-in-law, and daughter, among others in her audience. Susan and her cofounder had lost their husbands during the September 11 attacks.

After a few months under the shadow of trauma, they began raising money for the thousands of widows in Afghanistan who faced losing their children if they remarried. Under the marriage customs of their culture, when a widow remarries, her first set of children must return to their father's extended family. The widow carries herself into the new household and into her new husband's community alone, stripped of her children.

Within three months, Susan's small nonprofit was providing literacy classes for these women. By working with CARE and other nonprofits that had established access to the widows, a team of volunteers taught them how to market their skills, in order to live independently with their children. Susan even learned how to work beside the Taliban so that they would not eliminate by force the support being provided to these stranded women.

---

[1] If you distrust what I mean here, please read Ralph Waldo Emerson's brilliant essay "Fate," a short iteration of the themes of scarcity and frugality in a swift and severe world. Emerson wrote this five-part essay in the wake of his son Waldo's premature death. I find this to be Emerson's most worthwhile essay, in terms of modern stresses, because it is sincere, tough, and useful from line one to its end. Emerson offers us an operational theory of confronting our own fate.

A Reflection upon Reflection

I saw in Susan the strengths I had first seen in my mother. Although Susan is more articulate and better educated than my mom, the dynamic origin of this strength through trauma has a shared source. Susan Retik embodies posttraumatic growth; rather than being dominated by the real stress of her own trauma and tragedy, she increased social value by giving back. These extraordinary choices of growth are actually quite ordinary, as they are available to many. In fact, humans may be hardwired to learn by doing after trauma.

Many in my old neighborhood, meanwhile, remained behind, stuck under the hood, like a jack-in-the-box, by the weight of their neighborhoods over their heads. Before one can jump out of the box, he or she must examine this feeling of being captive and explore those limits. I have often spoken about the early pleasures that scarcity brought me. When facing scarcity, you have the opportunity to experience the full dimension of everything you have. You come to know each piece of reading material intimately; you reread the best parts many times; you inventory everything, from meals to your gym socks, because they matter.

Nonetheless, it is easy to feel like a jack-in-the-box, like a toy of sorts. Those who recognize your hidden promise do their best to wind you up, so you shoot out of the box, play that game of basketball before thousands, and then return to the box near the railroad tracks. Sometimes it feels as though all comfort lies in the box. Sometimes it feels the opposite, as though all good resides outside the neighborhood.

Some of us got out of this initial box and enjoyed a chance at college and shared a set of recurrent principles about fair competition, whereas others simply enjoyed sustained good luck.

Between these two states—fair competition and good luck—resides the great mystery of fate and good fortune. This chapter is a modern-day reflection on freedom and fate, the ultimate question for a well-spent life today and tomorrow.

To that end, this chapter explores the nexus of freedom and fate in terms of how you can achieve a sense of purpose and peace within yourself—despite grand resistance along the way.

Reasons on Top of Reflections

Good fortune was operating when I met the radically clear new economic thinker E. F. Schumacher in college. Schumacher set me free to think other thoughts than those within the dominant academic supply-side culture. One rich principle started me off correctly: "Think generously of the poor," Schumacher warned, "because they do so much with so little."

Schumacher's liberating work helped me leave behind those feelings of being a jack-in-the-box. In the spirit of this great economist's legacy, I will end this essay by considering what it takes to avoid more war and strife in the near future, and I will describe what we mean by *emotional intelligence* in business.

In my experience, these different but related themes construct an overarching point about freedom: although most of what we encounter involves large elements of luck and chance and fate, we often have enough room within our control to actually make a difference in our lives.

A Little Bird Called Fate

These early experiences of poverty and persistence sat on my head like a little bird, bringing a few good options to my life.

Like Franklin, I spent time trying to weed out my most serious imperfections—from tobacco and alcohol to drugs in sports. I knew I would need to get some weight off my shoulders, stand tall, and work my way out of poverty in order to find inventiveness. The next examples portray my sportive seriousness in contemplating this fate.

My first paying jobs involved washing cars from age 8 to 10. Then, during my teen years and summers of early college, I landscaped the higher-quality homes in my hometown and adjacent towns. I learned a great deal about sales, margin pricing, and the basics of enterprises in terms of staff and talent by selling up into wealthier neighborhoods. I accomplished all this before my formal study at Cornell.

This pattern of early competitive frugality matured as I went from high school to college to my first professional jobs. I was seldom idle; the markets kept me from establishing false pride, and my friends and family often kept me out of real trouble and folly. Soon enough, I received some stabilizing—and then depressing—opportunities in academia.

A Stranger in Paradise

I felt like a stranger in paradise during the 44 semesters I spent as a professor. In retrospect, the feelings are even more profoundly those of estrangement. From Cornell to Clarkson to Rensselaer Polytechnic Institute (RPI), I never felt fully at home in a leisure-class occupational setting. At these schools, I was still a jack-in-the-box but I lacked the right polish to shine. To the faculty, I was a bull in their china shop and to my acquaintances, often an embarrassment.

The great mass of professors—while absorbed in the toils of their research and the cares and activities of their lives—is only dimly conscious of the pace and the patterns of work that students pursue besides classwork. I, for example, wrote my first book, which was published in 1976, while an undergraduate, without much awareness among my professors. In addition, my stay in academia granted me both the time and the resources to develop my own approach to money, people, and rules. No professor cared about my attempt to meld this into a general operating philosophy. So I was free to roam, invent, refine, and try out, just as I had in youth. That was the institution's greatest gift to me: freedom from the factory work that many thought my first destiny.

Being restless, I engaged in other activities during those 44 semesters in limbo. I was a lobbyist during some of that time and was enterprising enough to build my firm and write my books during the years from 1981 to 2000.

It is not uncommon for professors at the better schools to have increasing writing, speaking, and consulting gigs as their reputations grow. Yet I was a bit different: I never felt at home in the leisure of these school settings. In fact, I left all faculty meetings and most of the classes I taught wanting nothing more than to get back to work.

It was good for me to have this daily contrast between theory and practice—but not good enough in the end. Thus, I admire people who aren't tied to a single revenue stream. In my experience, some of the most self-righteous are those who work for only one corporation or in journalism for only one outlet. Those single-stream professions become preoccupied and narrowed in their effort to remain pure. But academia granted the license for additional income and the structured chance to explore relationships well outside the box of my immediate professional appointments, simply because no one was looking. Senators liked talking to professors, as did the press.

A motto ran through my mind during most of those days in paradise—and especially after most tenure and promotion committee meetings: "Actors speak of imaginary things as if they are real; academics speak of real things as if they are imaginary." This is not true of the many exceptional professors changing the nature of research or making major technical contributions to society. But it is unfortunately true for many management school professors. I was often surprised, and then depressed, by how few actual classics sat on their shelves!

I was a stranger in paradise because I refused to accept fully the game of academic and peer-reviewed thought. Life—that world of events—had always been faster than my thoughts, so why should I fully trust the notions of success from peers only? In other words, my instincts to conserve, protect, and remain alert were stronger than my academic training. These rather than my Cornell training, were the source of my interest in taking intelligent risks.

Early trauma teaches you never to believe that the realm of thought can be faster than the world of event. My mom, Susan, and the many others who enjoy the benefits of post-traumatic growth know this. It empowers them to take risks and to be persistent every day. This is the very essence of existentialism: we are thrown into this world, and life doesn't stop until it stops. I find that many company founders share this mind-set when they start their firms. The same kinds of forces lodge in their active mind-set.

That is why I see all this as lucky. I just dove in and learned by doing. Yet the principles are now clear to me. And writing this makes the patterns sharper. I hope this is worthy of sharing with you and your most important generation.

The Financial Page on Start-Ups

My daughter asked me—rather intelligently—"How did you start a firm, Dad, when you had so little at the beginning? How did you have enough to start and then pay the folks you work with?"

The annals of *Inc.* magazine suggest that the theme of doing more with less dominates the financial pages of most start-ups and the early memories of many enterprisers. Bootstrapping an enterprise comes naturally for those who earn early attention, either in sports or on the street. Often those folks start, and never pause to get that master of business administration (MBA).

Even when earning less than $5,000 per year as a landscaper in high school, I saved at least 33 percent of that annual income, just in case. During my 10 years of study and while teaching for cash at Cornell, I spent far less than my scholarships, even after buying rooms full of books, enriching my mind with movies and plays, and indulging many times, with glee, in the joy of good friends. Benjamin Franklin's biographies are filled with details of how he blended frugality with pleasure and invention, as well as with friends.

Weeks after starting my firm in 1981, I assumed my first professorship at Clarkson University in inexpensive Potsdam, New York, and started saving in a grander fashion through Teachers Insurance and Annuity Association–College Retirement Equities Fund as soon as I was vested. I can recall signing the TIAA-CREF retirement papers in a basement and thinking about the money I would get so far into the future (a future that is now a mere 37 months away as I write this retrospect!).

This gave me my first taste of long-term planning; no matter how little you have in these accounts at the start, the money managers treat all clients at TIAA-CREF with interesting projections and attention. I now invite those in charge of governance of this $440 billion nest egg to speak at my leadership seminars. Why? Well, I think it is useful to have these long-term savers share their standards and oversight with my clients and corporate affiliates.

In retrospect, I suppose that some deans should have asked me whether I was double-dipping during those decades of multiple revenue streams, as I always found ways to supplement the meager salary one earns as a professor with outside sources.

Those other sources of revenue, which I disclosed earnestly to the general counsels of my schools, were writing and speaking gigs, consulting work for large and small firms, and some basic work as a stringer for a giant lobbying firm. Potsdam was a terribly small community, so I longed for the action of Washington, DC, assignments. In retrospect, I want the new generation to know how open the doors of power remain to you and the White House, if you know how to ask the right questions—efficiently and with respect.

For the first 20 years after I had received my PhD, my wife and I supported ourselves and lived according to Abraham Lincoln's idea that the only way to test the rigor of one's beliefs is to take "frequent public opinion baths" through public speaking. We wanted to test ourselves frequently outside of the secure compounds of academia, where the audiences are essentially captive markets.

Some semesters I'd be in Washington, DC, three times a month. I could meet my class demands and travel, thereby avoiding the idleness about which Franklin warned. I chose to teach Franklin's *Autobiography* for 10 years at Clarkson. His lines of his thinking were kind of hardwired into me by then.

Franklin gives your brain a kind of productive music. His aphoristic style resonates like a song, repeating the refrain that "you can do it"—a message that has real motivation and sensual stimulation behind it. This tonal support meant much to me, and still does.

When I ask some friends now if their life arc after college followed a similar stinginess, they laugh with the honesty that self-reflection allows. Some mention decades of spending 110 percent of what they earned, leaning on friends, family, or banks. Some spent 200 percent until checked by startled parents or partners.

In my first two professorships, tenure came fast; but my reluctance to feel secure (the opposite of folly, pride, and idleness) led me to deposit the maximum tax-deferred annuities each year. The key to doing more with less involves never feeling overly secure.

There is a difference between working under stress (a net modern bad) and working with intelligent worry (a life differentiator). A state of alertness helps us remain vigilant, like athletes with good starting statistics who keep bettering themselves over the years.

Over decades, watching other competitors tire or sell, I came to see my competitiveness in this larger context: we all walk on the beaches of fate, and as we age, maintaining our lifestyles becomes a chore mocked by many waves and insults. This is a visualization of what I felt even when young.

Life seemed short to me after losing my father. Watching my mother's home economics, I instructed myself to start saving now. This reluctance to feel secure is actually the opposite of anxiety. In my case, it is a stoic posture, a conscious decision path, not a psychological trauma.

For decades, I felt more real *not* being secure, proud, cocky, or a knucklehead. Our problem today involves systems much larger than the self. It is very difficult, but necessary, for leaders to achieve inventiveness in groups and frugality across nations. I can see how it is easier to overspend in government when debt remains distant from your own immediate well-being. Nonetheless, the patterns of personal spending and the spending of nations or corporations are, relatively speaking, the same. Debt, or excessive debt, comes from the same weakness in all forms of human organizations.

In contrast to the dips and gaps correlating spending to reserves, I had a vision one day, when I was about 10 years old, of a woman walking the beach alone with an umbrella. I did not know this woman but I could relate to her, bounced around by the waves and the wind. I believed that this image represented the control that I had of my fate, considering the raging sun, the ceaseless waves, and the salt in my wounds. So I determined to build myself a mental umbrella that could serve as a personal mantra (see Figure 4.1).

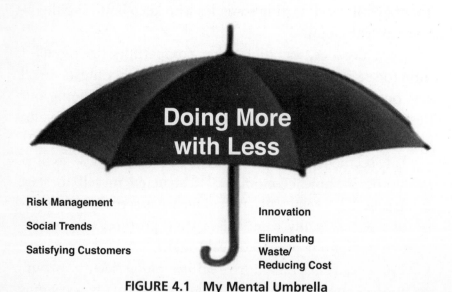

Doing More with Less

Risk Management

Social Trends

Satisfying Customers

Innovation

Eliminating Waste/ Reducing Cost

FIGURE 4.1 My Mental Umbrella

In retrospect, this umbrella mantra—however silly, however oversimplified—has helped me avoid the undertow of daily life ever since. I thank my mother for this fundamental worldview on frugality. She lived a life in poverty pretty well, with real civility and happiness. She helped me feel the connections between frugality and innovation. I realize now that those connections—all the things under one umbrella—are easily earned by individuals taking intelligent risks.

When Money Makes Money

Now, back to my savings—and those wonderful tax-deferred annuities. This approach allows you to win in two directions: tax reduction and compounded value over decades. I am not referring here to any specific instruments or account types, as no one can avoid the wisdom of basic diversification. I am simply returning us to the Franklin fundamental of early savings that compound. By the time I was in my mid-forties, I calculated that I had arrived at financial independence. I spoke to my wife about this discovery, evaluated the tensions of breaking from academe and its blankets of security, and then took the dive into total self-determination.

Sigmund Freud notes in *Civilization and Its Discontents*: "the voice of the intellect is a soft one, but after continual rebuffs, it shall be heard." What I heard during these early years was mostly my mother's voice.[2]

I have heard sneers through decades and felt the judgment in different corridors and times. I even reflect on all this today with a profound sense of good luck, as well as

---

[2] I say all this with some sense of the risk of appearing comfortable or smug or self-congratulatory. I realize that dropping names such as Benjamin Franklin and E. F. Schumacher in reference to one's life can be seen as comical by the sophisticated and as self-indulgent by the humble. I think, instead, that we learn through mimesis, basic imitation, and it matters immensely whom we choose to imitate.

some superstition about not upsetting the powers of fate with too much attention to these choices I have made. This is not meant to be bleak, but to state some existential facts that keep me writing, never satisfied with the margins of comfort I have earned.

It pays to reflect on how the discipline of managing one's life starts early. At age 10, when I saw that woman on the beach with that windswept umbrella, I already knew something significant about freedom and fate.

I knew by 10 years old that no one in my family could give me a margin of comfort if I did not earn it first myself. It is easy to think of running something on another person's money, but that comes with certain risks, risks as certain as bank interest or personal debt. Unfortunately, not many governments collectively share this natural distrust of debt. Politicians running government purse strings from America and England to Ireland and Greece to Africa and the former Soviet regions now need a simple kick in the pants: doing more with less means success for them.

Maybe because I had the good fortune of being born poor, I never trusted debt. I silently celebrated the power of compounded interest and tax deferral for my first six books, never saying a word—except to family—about how I was using my own savings to grow a firm. I certainly did not learn that at Cornell, where most of my friends had credit cards and ran smoothly on others' cash.

These savings allowed me to leave RPI at age 45. This was the second time I had given up tenure. I recalled both times Franklin's trepidation on leaving the comforts of his Massachusetts home for the uncertainties of Philadelphia and his printing press. By age 45, doing more with less was as much a habit for me as a principle.

But why did I leave academia?

Franklin had left his home and comfort zone partly out of anger at his brother. I did it partly out of anger at the feelings I had in academia. I wanted to leave a world of doing more *for* less and enter a world of doing more *with* less.[3]

I believed that those who hit their heads on the ceiling of certainty every day, yet do not leave, are the ones who might look a little comical in the end. Luckily, my wife of now more than three decades supported this adventure with stoic strength. In addition, I realize now that I left these comforts because I wanted to feel the full-time freedom of the firm I had founded. In the many years since I have left RPI, my firm has significantly increased its revenue, reputation, and relationships every year.

Was this due to hard work or fate?

I now have built a headquarters to avoid rent. I continue to trim and to mature our staff as we grow in global assignments with more impact and more freedom. This is a working definition of freedom for me. For me, a life under weekly if not constant tests and frequent public opinion baths is far better, far more fulfilling, than a life of leisure. You may ask, then, if this part of the book is limited to one principle, spending less. To that, I'd have to answer no.

What stayed constant was my love of people and my respect for frugality and freedom from serious debt, as well as my sense of how rules can be reshaped into creativity in times of stress and scarcity. In short, the making of the best teams begins with self-reliance.

---

[3] Recently, I started describing these pacesetting moves as no longer wanting to be a jack-in-the-box. You can hear, with sharp journalists asking the questions, about the challenges I faced at www.davidgibbons.org and at www.SmallBusinessAdvocate.com. Here I explain these transitions from security into business innovation, in an interactive recording of radio shows.

Beyond the Founder Syndrome

So many firms stop growing in their third to fifth decades, limited by the personalities and preferences of their founders and friends. We felt this prelude to stagnation, as well. For me, the answer resided in figuring out the complex that exists between freedom and fate. One of my friends, Marc Strauss, a very successful businessman, notes that "Every firm has a birth, a maturing, and an aging like in life. . . . The trick is to extend life and its enjoyments by giving." In the second to fourth decade of my firm, there were times I had to tie my fate to the ship of others for proper buoyancy and lift. I had to concede freedoms and transform them into the intensity of group action.

Thus, I now want to turn your attention away from my life to focus on the life of one of my mentors, E. F. Schumacher.

A life in business is usually a composite story of multiple influences. Schumacher's work convinced me, at a critical point in the development of the AHC Group, that I could grow a firm without debt, despite what the banks wanted to offer me. And more important, he suggested—in concept at least—that being small in size could allow one to be big in impact and purpose. I found that appealing in terms of freedom and fate. I centered my venture ego (the ego required to found a company) on this idea of a beautiful smallness, avoiding the need for significant splats of venture money.

Too often an MBA starts a business plan with a debilitating giantism at its core. Schumacher taught me how to base my firm's use of science, accounting, taxes, human talent, and outsourcing on the frugal idea that people matter as much as rules and dollars. Manipulating rules and leveraging debt can prove demanding, while liberating the competitive and frugal impulses in dear colleagues can be much less expensive. An economics based on people allows this fundamental realignment of money, people, and rules.

A Life Story

When E. F. Schumacher visited the Cornell University campus in the late 1970s, he made a strange request that I'll never forget. He wanted to speak in Sage Chapel, the old redbrick sanctuary at the center of the campus, not far from the submerged bookstore. I was an undergraduate who had stumbled upon Schumacher's book at the college bookstore, and I did not know then how smart he was in choosing this setting at Sage. At the time, Sage was seldom frequented by my schoolmates, but I found it calming and often empty, and I'd often read and study there, apart from the crowds at the Union across the street.

To my surprise, when Schumacher started speaking, Sage was full. Hundreds were mesmerized. I left Sage on that cool fall night in Ithaca, New York, feeling changed. Most everything Schumacher said, from his critique of large organizations, to his love of the poor, sounded right to me. I found a mentor in Schumacher that improved my practice.

The next week I wrote my first published book review, a naïve glorification of Schumacher's *Small Is Beautiful*. I still appreciate the grace and power of his mind and the lasting value of his commonsense approach to technology, economics, and science. I picked up this book again after the horrific terrorist attacks of September 11 and found both solace and insight in those pages he had first shared with the world in 1973.

Across time, E. F. Schumacher has influenced many social reform pragmatists, from Amory B. Lovins of the Rocky Mountain Institute to those who are now decoupling energy consumption from the health of economies around the world from Turkey to Southeast Asia. Over the last few years I can see his fingerprints in my understanding of how invention and frugality make peace with the world.

Telling the Truth

Schumacher had that rare gift of telling simple truths, without the wind and smoke of sophistication or any excess of professionalism. You can see Schumacher's redemptive imagination at work in concepts such as products "designed to serve the human person" and in the many forms of his concept of "technology with a human face." His bold plainness on the proper alignment of money, people, and rules is worth rereading if you are seeking some training in the higher principles of how global economies will work.

Schumacher's insights into the modern world are more appropriate for the twenty-first century than for his own era. He was about 60 years ahead of his time. He is Benjamin Franklin all over again, although a classic British citizen. The following passage became a part of my original vision statement, when I founded the AHC Group in 1981:

> The structure of the organization can then be symbolized by a man holding a large number of balloons in his hand. Each of the balloons has its own buoyancy and lift, and the man himself does not lord it over the balloons, but stands beneath them, yet holding all the strings firmly in his hand. Every balloon is not only an administrative but also an entrepreneurial unit.

This sums up the nature of our group's senior associates, where former chief executive officers of BP America, executive lawyers from Kimberly-Clark and General Motors, and former heads of Whirlpool and Canada's largest energy firm, now work on our company accounts with efficiency and impact. You can learn more about this astounding set of senior associates in my firm at www.AHCGroup.com.

A Man Holding Balloons

I've grown my firm doing more with less each year by keeping clearly in mind this image of the man holding balloons. It does not take a massive headquarters to do what we do; we are highly decentralized, and we are interlinked across countries and regions.

In retrospect, I was simply competitive and frugal. I did not want to be seduced by the appeal of size and debt and the mandates of many managing partners. I took the best from the best, and I redeployed.

You can do the same. I owe my friends Franklin and Schumacher a great deal, in fact and in practice, each day. They gave me so much for so little. As a result I never needed to pay for an MBA, a law degree, or much advertising, even though some of the world's best attorneys and business executives work with us.

Today's More Dangerous World

We need to be more competitive in today's world, not less, because it is so much swifter than Franklin's world and so much more severe than Schumacher's. Only you can adapt the tools and principles to the new social needs of today.

Our business schools, however, are preparing students to be *less* competitive. I have observed that graduates of business schools, after three years of MBA training, become large-system optimizers without any practical experience in change management and leveraging social value. They do not become Pat Mahoneys. They borrow before they truly invent. They are insufficiently enterprising, in other words. They can talk it but do not walk it. At times, I have seen MBAs more stupid about business than before business school. They rapidly fall into debt after graduation.

In many ways future cars, homes, and computers will be designed by doing more with less gas, less energy, and fewer metals (see Chapter 6). With these guides about why small is beautiful before you, you should be able to navigate the swift currents of free choice and fate more ably, without destabilizing debts.

This reflection on my lifework, then, has given me a reason to rethink frugality's unstoppable significance for tomorrow. The approach we advocate is good for your lifestyle, your wealth creation, and the net good of our global society.

While Franklin and Schumacher may help frame the house of your future thinking, you still need to proceed by bringing new value in the mix. This is not armchair science, but a new way to wealth.

Relating Different Lives

Human identity is the synthesis of many good and bad experiences; I believe human identity is best and most productive when derived from many competing sources. I have argued that the same goes for productivity and balance in a firm. If everyone in the firm is a corporate attorney, your firm will not be inventive. If all are risk managers, you will not understand the benefits of risk. And if some of you know how to make a product, but not sell it, you will fail.

Far too many forces seek like-mindedness in a firm, which weighs down a firm in time and produces what I call machine-like MBAs. Many MBAs I have met, or who have applied to work at the AHC Group, are mistrained to think of my firm as if it were a yacht, mathematically destined to go faster and further if you jettison some goods from it or add a smarter crew.

This is simply absurd, if compared to the role of frugality and the deliberate smallness of my boat! A company of people is not a machine. In contrast, I often look for more figurative balloons, for more socially responsive and innovative types, and I then measure their buoyancy within our group almost weekly; I change teams as needed to ascend peaks and offer freedoms that are rare in competing firms that I benchmark. Successful firms find values in weightless leadership that propels them into the near future; cost cutting and staff reduction are too mechanical a fix to really matter in a big way over time.

This streamlined portfolio approach of the AHC Group has meant much to me. Now I see this hedging to streamline may become more commonplace with time. To put all your eggs in one firm's nest egg is no longer wise.

My point here is that my firm is a synthesis of Franklin, Schumacher, and so many others. What matters in the end are the principles worthy of sharing, as noted at www.AHCGroup.com.

The concepts that will prevail from this book have more to do with your habits and beliefs than with mine. I do not expect you to read the books that I have read, nor do I expect for you to do the things that I've found of value. But I *do* expect you to be moved to action. You will have arrived when you choose to remain in the game for the future without losing your footing in humanity. We end this chapter on freedom and fate with a fateful question: How can your life contribute toward the next golden age?

War and Want, Freedom and Peace

And now, in conclusion, here is my short reflection on war and peace.

You may all recall that Benjamin Franklin was involved in a most fateful war: the War of Independence. You may also recall that E. F. Schumacher ran the British Coal Board during World War II. So both my mentors, and in fact my father, knew about the military and military ways. My mother often used to joke that I would either become a factory worker, like herself, or a warrior.

My war was with life itself, and how easy it is to waste it.

I believe that when we are put up against the walls of fate, we choose our path consciously—either in the posture of a warrior or of one wanting to create some social value. Most business lingo celebrates business as warfare, which is really the wrong metaphor. Let's apply this thinking to today's political landscape as we close.

Uprisings Today and Tomorrow

Vast unrest in the Arab world may seem like a singular phenomenon, a historical wave that crashes and then recedes. But it begs the question of whether we can avoid the fate of war by addressing the tangle of social need. With Earth soon to host 7 billion people, we would be naïve to neglect a twenty-first-century reality: the basic human struggle for freedom, food, and energy will intensify on a global scale over the next few decades. As I am writing this book, riots over rising food prices have emerged, and this year's resurgent inflation of prices at gas stations and grocery stores suggests more trouble ahead. In short, we live in a global greenhouse surrounded by both swift and severe market forces.

We in the West have typically responded to the needs of growing populations through ingenuity in the service of more: *more* corn per acre, *more* big-box stores (and stunningly large grocery stores), *more* personal and corporate wealth, and *more* everything. History suggests one thing: this works—until it doesn't. War also works—until it doesn't.

And it is clear today that the features of Franklin's and Schumacher's works that were most easily forgotten have to do with being diplomatic, rather than warlike. Franklin's wit and wisdom about self-determination and competitive frugality amount to much more than self-help talking points. His appreciation of how historic changes brought on a war that separated him from his son and wife are well-studied and worth remembering—but often forgotten in the heat of the moment. In addition, Schumacher's decision to spend the years after World War II talking about how to guide those who were perplexed by war is worth our concern, at a time when America is expected to police the rest of the world, which is in so much turmoil.

At this point in human history, the only world war we should be fighting is the one to temper our own excessive competitiveness.

To sum up our argument to this point—we must be more competitive than in the past, but only in terms of inventiveness. We must eliminate the kind of competitiveness that thrives on making enemies.

What do I mean by that?

First, it is harder to develop an identity that is stable through peace than to develop one based on fear and prejudice and enemy formation. You can see the war on terror through these eyes; that much is well established. We go into games wanting to defeat our opponents as if they were real enemies. We go into television debates on national interests as if wars were the preferred options. We go into our firms expecting to eliminate the competition. The instinct is primal. The counterforce of diplomatic grace is the only available balance to the kind of competitive habits that say "you are either with me or against me."

Let me approach this first by life stories, my own being very much about a set of conscious decisions to shut down warring factions in myself, my family, and my neighborhood. And that is not circumstantial. I believe the war at home is ever present and almost irrepressible. In the larger world of scarcity, many warring factions will arise. Many families are consumed by this warring for attention. (Just open any issue of *Worth* magazine to read stories about the estate and inheritance wars of today.) In addition, it is human in any dispute to think of oneself as right, the one chosen, the one favored.

Early in life, I found that the trick to escaping these jack-in-the-box captivities is learning how to make peace first with the few captive options. This enabled me to keep more, waste less, and fight for another day. You can connect this line of motivated reasoning to competing on frugality, as it wastes less to not fight. This in fact is a higher social principle. Thomas Jefferson called this principle "commerce for peace."

Those who study emotional intelligence (EI) speak about its upside. This view proves more valuable in most societies than IQ or material inheritance or material advantage. The zeal of EI, its self-determination and persistence, outlasts initial disadvantages and material circumstances. Yes, this is very important, indeed. The human story is about shaping valued growth through adventure, not just about mounting material advantages.

The great books of cultural and material history, such as Jared Diamond's best seller *Guns, Germs, and Steel: The Fates of Human Societies*, miss the point about individuals and small teams shaping cultures and history. A material cultural historian such as Diamond tends to focus on the advantages of materials and resources at the expense of individual impact on history. The impact of restraint is hard to measure, but it is often priceless. Think here of Joan of Arc. In addition, individual social and executive leaders take the day, and this culture of personal success through group frugality seems even more abundant this century than last.

Therefore, we must fill the cup of our social impacts with EI, as well as calculated individual- and team-based business risk. EI is nothing unless in action. This gets me to a larger and higher social fact.

The pursuit of frugality itself may be the most elegant form of human aggression, as it entails the actions and the substance of both long-distance runners and saints. These folks are constructive, not destructive. Why have we forgotten so much of these principles in modern warfare?

Anyone who is competitive knows early on the strength of the primal need to fight or flee that is in all of us. All competitors liberate this inner drive and zeal, but some shape it into art, not war. Some spend it on result, not desolation.

The Value in Stoic Restraint

My life story involves consciously making decisions to shut down and repress the desire for escalating competition into warfare within both my teams and myself. I consciously pursued an alternative, softer path. This must be the way of our near future.

I now see more clearly than ever that my surrogate fathers Franklin and Schumacher suggested a new form of competitiveness in me. This was based on an approach—half masculine and perhaps half feminine—that allowed the thrill of adventure but not the taking of booty in war. I found this new form of adventure pleasurable because it was primarily inward—toward frugality, independence, creativity, and inward peace—rather than outward in conquest.

My friends in the Department of Defense, or my defense contractor clients, are probably saying at this point, "Easy for you to say, Bruce." But my point is that this last part of my story was not easy at all.

In a time of emerging globalization, it is far less challenging to compete in terms of nationalism in a time of emerging globalization and far easier to take sides than to resolve social capital matters. It is not easy at all, in fact, to go for peaceful resolution. When you have an industrial problem, it's far simpler to just bring out the bigger guns, the lobbying team, the public relations firms, and the trade group than it is to rework the product or the strategy.

And once we get 7 billion citizens on Earth, we need a golden age of innovation and peace because we cannot afford more war.

I am not claiming for a single minute that we can avoid all war; nor do I fantasize responsibly that we can temper patriotic gore. What I am saying is that a higher set of needs now exists and calls for a different set of leadership skills, similar to those first championed by Benjamin Franklin and E. F. Schumacher after their experiences of war.

The warring impulse leads to certain kinds of technical innovation—from titanium night optics to the extreme forms of information technology now utilized in drones to carry out remote warfare. This kind of innovation is well known in the medical and aerospace industries. Although less well known to most people, technical innovation as a result of war has also spilled over into industries dealing with chemicals, oil and gas, transportation, and automaking.

I expect that those who can make stealth bombers can also make more sustainable uses of water, oil, plastics, and pharmaceuticals. You simply must choose to turn the adventure in a different direction. The next golden age will be more of an inward journey than the great adventures of the last three centuries. Now is a time for inward growth.

Within my own life story is the emergence of social response capitalism (see Chapter 5 for details about this concept). Within my concepts of social response capitalism is a notion of greater peace, more sustained prosperity, and the inner adventure we feel when fulfilled.

Coda

I began this chapter by claiming that personal growth is too often forgotten as a feature of posttraumatic stress. In a parallel vein, I find that the ability to throttle the violent or aggressive urges within myself increases with age, experience, and reflection. Will this also prove possible over time with more and more satisfied consumers?

America emerged last century as an exceptional nation. In Europe, and in much of Asia, there was the feeling for centuries that behind every son was his father. When the first Adams of

America emerged, we began to say that each father had sons and daughters capable of a brighter future. Today, many wonder if we are declining back into a more stagnant, less open set of diminished expectations and diminished inheritances. I find that unlikely. The entire motivated reasoning behind doing more with less is to question the inevitability of decline.

You can get to normal benefits through frugality and innovation, but it takes a new worldview to achieve the golden age we seek. Once we truly become world citizens, the obligation to be diplomatic and inventive become supreme.

I now have friends in Istanbul who think this way about competing for sustainability; I have friends in Canada, Costa Rica, Japan, and South Korea who wish to do more with less. I may not live long enough to know, for sure, if this is a lasting trend or an informed fantasy. My life story so far—supported by the wealth of many shelves of good reading—suggests that phenomenon of a golden age has happened before and will happen again.

The difference is that now the great adventure comes from the pursuit of frugality and diplomacy rather than conquest and war.

PART

Near the Future

This world is not conclusion.
A Sequel stands beyond,
Invisible as music,
But positive as sound.

—Emily Dickinson

5

An Idler in the City

Capitalism Is Where We Live

When you have bought one fine thing, you must buy 10 more, that your appearance may be all of a piece; but Poor Dick says, 'It is easier to suppress the first desire than to satisfy all that follow it.' And it is as truly folly for the poor to ape the rich, as for the frog to swell, in order to equal the ox.

—Benjamin Franklin, *The Way to Wealth*

A survey of the key megacities of the world—from Athens to Paris and Istanbul to Tokyo—proves the need for new forms of leadership in a world constrained by carbon, capital, and the very nature of capitalism. As waters rise near Manhattan and our most ancient coastal megacities, new forms of competition must emerge and thrive. We must humanize more and agitate less as we near our shared future. The family of humans requires it.

Looking Back—and Looking Ahead

When I turned 40, I decided to adopt an open, fun-loving—you might say Whitmanesque—attitude toward business travel. Global journeys had become so mean, so difficult and encumbered, mainly owing to the checks and insults we have built to deter terrorism, that I had to summon up patience and add an extra day at each end, to visit the cities before and after I worked in them. This chapter grew out of those idle days away from home. I became an idler in the great cities.

I have visited a third of the top 100 megacities of this world over the last two decades. Each had a marvelously different feel, an inherent personality: Some were warm and exciting; others, troubling and suffocating. Yet they also share some common traits—the first of which is that they are *growing*. Franklin often cautioned individuals to control their desires, but he seldom scolded cities for their growth. This is an important realization to keep in mind in terms of our shared near future.

Second, these cities are being shaped by a set of swift social and corporate forces in distinct ways that are often overlooked or simply ignored. This gives us a chance to retest the fundamental principles of management and self-discovery examined in this book.

Consider why cities such as Athens, Paris, and London feel so appealing, whereas Istanbul and Tokyo feel so large and oppressively overwhelming. What challenges individuals in the great sprawls of poverty known as Shanghai, São Paulo, and Mumbai? What unseen forces are controlling and reshaping these cities: local or federal governments, well-financed nongovernmental organizations, the Gates Foundation, or the global press? What provides the engine of their sustained growth? Key patterns are clear, if you slow the pace of your travel.

I do not pretend to be able to answer these questions fully. Rather, this chapter is meant to start the debate within your own journeys, within the notes you take for yourself in your world travels. As Emily Dickinson says, "This world is not conclusion. A Sequel stands beyond, Invisible as music, But positive as sound."

I offer in this chapter a journeyman's set of observations about the growing relationship between cities and capitalism; in doing so, I ask if these connections jive with your lived experience of cities, as well as your sense of things to come.

For whatever the recent uprisings in the Middle East bring to all of us, and whatever we can expect next from our investments in the rapidly developing parts of China, Brazil, and the Asian tigers, we can be sure that urban changes will bring more capitalism rather than less to our near future. Figure 5.1 shows the megatrend in megacities in a nutshell.

After envisioning the overall trends in these megacities, you may see a modest suggestion that this new century will prove different—and luckier—than anyone supposed. In short, you can expect to see the signs of a more frugal golden

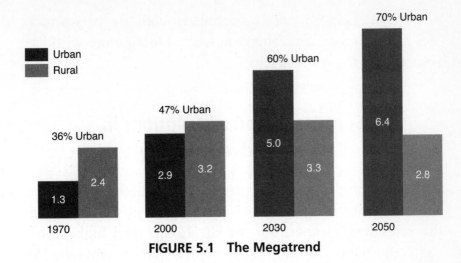

FIGURE 5.1   The Megatrend

age first taking shape in cities, both near and far. Never before was this mix of global competitiveness and urban frugality even possible.

Out of the informed optimism that capitalism brings to most cities, I sense a new architectonics of the near future. In this chapter, we explore how cities are better than both sports and most senior management teams in checking knuckleheads. Cities are severe and relentless that way.

Whether you are searching for a parking spot or watching your pocketbook, urban life, although remarkably more tolerant of diverse ideas and approaches in general than rural life, compels people to become more frugal, inventive, and diplomatic—in order to survive. Sure, urban life also allows abundant excess and visible consumptive exhibitionism. But I am writing about the aggregated trend, not the aggravating few.

Many of you know from experience how easy it is to drop a grand in two days in Manhattan unless you carry your Benjamin Franklins carefully. I have heard informed consumers alert their kids that a hundred is really a fifty in New York. Wait until they get to Tokyo or the ultrarich sections of Latin

megacities. These trends and scenes embody the new principles I preach for management at work. Doing more with less
is success in today's megacity.

Surprise, Surprise: Solutions in Competitive Frugality

The great and lasting megacities such as Athens, Paris, New
York, London, Sydney, and Calgary have evolved through
the relentless competition for the higher and higher efficiencies of labor, resources, and capital that are embodied in
global capitalism. I am not claiming these efficiencies lead
to paradise, smarter citizens, or better policy for our near
future. I am simply observing a major fact in how efficiency
comes about.

These cities are open to innovative change, to personal
diversity, and to expert inputs from afar. They compete on the
edge, a place where the demand for quality, price, style, and
social response unite. They aspire to host the Olympics, as
well as festivals, both musical and athletic. One can find them
on the map of the great rock 'n' roll tours. And most significantly, they are all teeming with the logic of advanced capitalism, from the multispeed world of Asia (witness Singapore
or the new coastal cities of China) to the mature economies of
Europe and North America. The competitive and the frugal
thrive in these cities.

Of course, no city is perfect.

It was not so long ago that the suburbs of Paris erupted
in riots. London is choking with automobiles and on-the-
street drinkers. Athens alone holds half the population of the
6,000 Greek islands, and my Greek translator talks of daily
congestion that chokes. But in general, the great cities have

embraced globalization in a more intelligent way than the rest. They are going global and going greener at the same time.

This collective intelligence about fair competition seems to be based on the history of populations rather than on religious or cultural beliefs, more on physical facts than on anything else. The top megacities, for example, display a remarkable and vast range of cultures and religious traditions that are responding to the pressure of rapidly increasing populations. Think of any megacity in India or Southeast Asia, and you'll see a massive range of differences coexisting between capitalism and beliefs.

In contrast, regarding those megacities that are suffering, it strikes me now that this group intelligence about the need to do more with less is being repressed by the few in power, with reactionary intent. It strikes me that those with reactionary intents are not facing these overriding facts; instead, they are feeling highly threatened by these sustainability challenges. The inevitable pressures on megacities will bring about change in the end. Here think of Libya and the great prerevolutionary Egyptian cities such as Cairo, where a few hundred families owned the vast majority of food, shelter, land, and educational resources. Here group intelligence for frugality was repressed for decades, until the recent uprisings. In sharp contrast, Figure 5.2 displays competition within the oil giants, where nation-states and multinationals continually check out the weak and prosper incredibly by being competitive.

Competitive frugality threatens to change those repressive regimes. Look at how rapidly this global competitiveness, what I called the S Frontier in my book *World Inc.* (www .WorldIncBook.com), has shifted the ownership structures of the oil giants, for example. I can assure you that these relative numbers will be vastly different in a matter of years, not centuries, as is generally the case when nations change their

Anglo-Persian Oil Company	Now named BP
Royal Dutch Shell	Operates Shell brand
Standard Oil of California	Now named Chevron
Standard Oil of New Jersey	Now named Exxon; acquired Mobil to become ExxonMobil
Standard Oil Company of New York	Became Mobil; Then Acquired by Exxon
Gulf Oil	Acquired by Chevron
Texaco	Acquired by Chevron

FIGURE 5.2   The Seven Sisters and Their Fates

basic orientation. This is why I see social response capitalism as embedded in a swift and severe S Frontier.

I predict that over time historians will call these structural changes in economic systems the beginning of the rules of a golden age. No one is expert enough to claim they fully know these new rules of globalization yet. But the trend is clear. Overall, energy price volatility and urban designs favor—in the billions of decisions required each week—a world full of people who are more frugal, inventive, inclusive, and diplomatic.

Another way to phrase this: watch how large concentrations of people share looser and looser rules as capitalist policies open up borders, enabling people to make money near each other despite their vast differences.

If capitalism continues to uproot the remaining repressive regimes, as in the last four to six decades (and especially during the Arab uprisings of 2011), many believe a more compassionate world might evolve. You can now find these thoughts not only among social progressives such as George Soros but also among the Heritage Foundation scholars.

It is naïve to suggest that the ascent of social response capitalism will take a simple linear path. Vicious battles will be fought from region to region, and tyrants can and will rebunker themselves in certain regions (witness North Africa's top cities today, from Tripoli to Cairo). Yet I suspect that many of those left standing in the next decades will exhibit the management and self-determining principles, behaviors, and policies outlined in this book.

Pause and contemplate this new global openness: it resides in a better alignment of money, people, and rules. I believe that this new openness has been brought about by the concentration of people in one larger neighborhood, and that this process requires new and more frugal competition. I am not saying we can do away with the world's Walden Ponds, for we all need our sanctuaries. I am not saying that people of plenty have entirely ceased to dominate. I am simply saying watch how the principles of this book support and inform the existing urbanization trends inherent in social response capitalism.

Megacompanies Sculpting Megacities

How will these large megacities—and the megacompanies that they house (companies such as Hewlett-Packard [HP], General Electric [GE], Exxon Mobil, Shell, and Google)— address our urban needs as every region of the world begins to encounter severe carbon and capital constraints? Are these places mobilizing a response to poverty and disease, crowding and mobility? Are they rebalancing humanity's needs for money, people, and rules?

The best of these megacities are embracing more public transportation and learning to do more with less. They are preparing for an overpopulated world, with constraints on capital and carbon.

Those who are aware of the threat of rising waters caused by excess carbon in our atmosphere have already begun climate-change mitigation projects. The new $15 billion, 245-mile water-control system surrounding New Orleans is a climate-change mitigation project. Similar plans are under way in Venice. Firms such as Architecture, Engineering, Consulting, Operations, and Maintenance (AECOM), CH2MHill, and Arcadis, all massive, globe-spanning engineering corporations, have made billions in those cities through competitive frugality profiting from doing more with less.

This is the good news. Since World War II, change toward frugality has often occurred outside of federal policy. The race for frugality is not restricted by nation-state boundaries. It is a force derived from the liberalization inherent in technology and in the opening of global markets characteristic of our times.

I have come to see these changes as based on the higher facts of physical history. Once you comprehend frugality not only as a personal virtue but as one that is essential in a world filled with 7 billion souls, you'll get what I mean.

I predict that a great rebalancing will take place in most megacities by 2025. Total oil production, for example, has declined 4.5 percent annually over the last three years. This is the prime force requiring the rebalancing, but there are many other social factors as well, including population growth. As a result of stressing elements in social history, the push for unconventional sources of oil and gas, such as the oil sands in Canada and natural gas fracking across many nations, is rapidly being felt in many regions of the world.

What are we to make of all of this, relative to the fate of individuals and our great cities, who are so dependent on cars, oil, and computing?

My firm has several clients working to make sure that the companies producing these new forms of energy will share a socially acceptable code of best practices. I find my clients coming around to the fundamental principles laid out in this book, and they can see how scarcity, frugality, innovation, and diplomacy relate.

As a result of these developments, expect a set of established and transparent codes of industrial behavior to emerge rapidly in a set of megacities showing high rates of population growth. This is the way to our near future. Our need for energy, food, and shelter will redefine our rules so that they march more rapidly toward these arts of competitive frugality.

You can cut to the essence of this question about the great lag in national and state policies by asking the question about sustainability in reverse. One way is to ask the question: "Do the 600 largest companies situate their goods and their talent in the center of these megacities?" The answer is a resounding *no*.

Although the motives of these giants are complex and nimble, their social behavior has visible consequences. They buy space in suburban Naperville, rather than downtown Chicago. HP is located outside of Heathrow Airport, not in downtown London. You find the world's largest fertilizer firm, Agrium, just beyond the limits of downtown Calgary, near a supermarket and a movie theater in a residential neighborhood. Many of these powerhouses are clients of my firm, so I get to visit their offices and make 40- to 80-minute commutes from the airport. Their location is a capitalist's logic.

The pattern is now almost a commonplace fact among the 600 largest organizations that my firm tracks. Corporate giants—from Toyota, Google, and HP to Exxon Mobil, Shell, and Walmart—know how to pick cheaper, more frugal, and better locations, extending the center city into a megacity and drawing talent, resources, and innovation after them. Many have asked if this is a net good. I ask: How can we call this anything but the relentless logic of social response capitalism (SRC)? (Again, please see www.WorldIncBook.com for a full explanation of this SRC set of developments.)

I believe that the changes in this new century boil down to two related things: globalization in more efficient goods and services and our shared sustainability demands. You see both when you look at our needs in terms of food, transportation, and dwellings in a smaller world—and you cannot have one without the other. We need both sustainability and people-based globalization. Getting the best of both resides in competition and frugality.

This is what William Throop, the provost of Green Mountain College, meant when he said, "The global benefit of frugality is that it moves our emphasis from financial capital to social capital." He further refined his claim by noting how frugality enters the city and commerce as "a rich means to buffer individualism by building and maintaining robust social networks." You see this in the jazz clubs in any megacity, in the schools, even in the Starbucks. Humans, when surrounded by many other humans, become alert to social networks and social capital. Economies based on this type of exchange are very different from those based on farming.

Although many articulate critics of urbanization lament this cultural development, I see it as the blue sky of hope and resourcefulness amid the clouds of sprawl. Of course, I, too, hate the waste inherent in ribbon developments. To quote

Throop again, "The real social dimension in competing on sustainability is that it gives the world a problem-solving disposition." This kind of urban encounter helps humans learn how to develop the capacity to draw things out of a group and achieve the wisdom of teams.

You can question whether it is right, or all for the best, but you cannot really question why rising populations and the corporate race to efficiency fit together in megacities like a hand in a glove. Maybe it is better to think of them as active and engaged sisters.

There is something incredibly rapid and shocking about global consolidation: Things grow exponentially overnight. Each week, one large company merges with another; one city unites with its neighbor. Although we see it happen all the time, we don't exactly know what it means.

I once shared a short elevator ride in Washington, DC, with a senator from an oil state; he actually had his aide press the "stop" button so that we could continue our quick conversation. As we discussed this global tendency toward consolidation, he said, "Certainly, the seven sisters—the world's largest oil players—must be doing something right to get that big. It couldn't just be their love of debt, their faith in complex technologies, and their thirst to span the globe. They must be doing something right, don't you think?" (See Figure 5.2.)

Knowing how far his tenure and his reach were financed by energy and infrastructure, we opened the elevator doors in a state of polite disagreement. Yet his force opened my eyes regarding competition among giants.

I've been pondering this question for 15 years now, since I visited most of these oil giants. Of those original seven, only four remain. My firm has worked for three of these top four over the last decade, week in and week out. Yet overall, I still ask: Is this rapid expansion of companies a result of doing things right? And what exactly does the senator mean by *right?* Is it right in terms of money or people's privileges? Or does he mean right in terms of the rules of fair competition?

I cannot begin to answer these important questions on equity. However, I think you will see that there is something right about the hand-and-glove relationship that has emerged between most megacities and capitalism—something that goes much deeper than shared fashions. We are exploring here the nature of cities after we reach peak oil, and we are investigating social trends: what happens to our consumption rates once we have more people than arable land.

Corporate Culture and Megacities

Consider these statistics. Our consulting practice now treats the following four higher facts as basic as physics and as immutable as waves pounding a seashore:

1. Of the 100 largest economies in the world, 56 are not nations. They are huge, Earth-spanning corporations, often working in more than 115 nations. From Copenhagen to Caracas, these firms exist around the globe now, not just in nation-states. You find the associated brands and products in all megacities. Diageo, for example, has its beverages in over 112 counties, controlling a dozen of the world's best recognized brands, from Guinness to Baileys.

2. The 100 largest multinational corporations (MNCs) now control about 22 percent of global foreign assets. These are household names, including Google, HP, Walmart, Toyota, and Shell. Most children today are more familiar with these names than with the names of nations or states.

My own daughter, for example, knew what HP was before she knew the periodic table, although she excelled in advanced biology!

3. Three hundred MNCs now account for at least a third of the world's total assets. Some economists in my group, using a set of outside sources, have reconfirmed these figures since I wrote *World Inc.* (www.WorldIncBook.com). For the first time in human history, Earth-spanning organizations are shaping massive markets and influencing trends, far in advance of government rules.

4. More than 44 percent of world trade now occurs within these top multinationals, up from the trends first reported in *World Inc.* (2007). These trends clearly grow along with the megacities, and this chapter demonstrates the consequences.

If we think of global commerce as slices in a shared pizza pie, you can see how many of the slices are already devoted to business-to-business exchange, rather than to regional policy questions or the tax and safety concerns of nation-states. Immense business consequence, and the fate of so many lives, resides in these transfers of population among cities noted, for example, in Figure 5.3.

And herein can be unearthed the new grounds for hope in social response capitalism. In the end, B2B, or business-to-business, strategies (something my small group has excelled at in the past 22 years) can be more frugal than federal policy. Since B2B is inherently more competitive, seeking efficiencies and swift deals among the nimble and huge, it is often done before direct changes in government work and rules.

Think here about Google, Walmart, and GE, and most any of the Fortune 500 companies. B2B is the way of the world,

Population 2007   **Population 2025**

1. Tokyo **35.7m**	**36.4m** 1. Tokyo
2. Mexico City **19.0m**	**26.4m** 2. Mumbai
3. New York-Newark **19.0m**	**22.5m** 3. Delhi
4. Sao Paulo **19.0m**	**22.0m** 4. Dhaka
5. Mumbai **18.8m**	**21.4m** 5. Sao Paulo
6. Delhi **15.9m**	**21.0m** 6. Mexico City
7. Shanghai **15.0m**	**20.6m** 7. New York-Newark
8. Kolkata **14.8m**	**20.6m** 8. Kolkata
9. Buenos Aires **12.8m**	**19.4m** 9. Shanghai
10. Dhaka **13.5m**	**19.1m** 10. Karachi
11. Los Angeles-Long Beach-Santa Ana **12.5m**	**16.8m** 11. Kinshasa
	15.8m 12. Lagos
12. Karachi **12.1m**	**15.6m** 13. Cairo
13. Rio de Janeiro **11.9m**	**14.8m** 14. Manila
14. Osaka-Kobe **11.7m**	**14.5m** 15. Beijing
15. Cairo **11.3m**	**13.8m** 16. Buenos Aires
16. Beijing **11.1m**	**13.7m** 17. Los Angeles-Long Beach-Santa Ana
17. Manila **11.1m**	
18. Moscow **10.5m**	**13.4m** 18. Rio de Janeiro
19. Istanbul **10.1m**	**12.4m** 19. Jakarta
	12.1m 20. Istanbul
	11.8m 21. Guangzhou
	11.4m 22. Osaka-Kobe
	10.5m 23. Moscow
	10.5m 24. Lahore
	10.2m 25. Shenzhen
	10.1m 26. Chennai

FIGURE 5.3   The World's Megacities

controlling your choice points and your day as a consumer in this vast universe of goods. Yet how many times today have you even thought about B2B? It is a kind of quiet change, a bloodless revolution, to those outside of big business.

Once we have adjusted our attitudes to deal with this new frontier—in which corporations, not nation-states, are ascendant—we will find that this new, globalized world can help improve our cars and our homes; our computers and our appliances; our food and our health; and the length, comfort, and satisfaction of our lives.

But do corporations always do this? Absolutely not. We know that many are shortsighted, concerned merely with short-term wins, and often voracious in their growth spurts. But they do something to cities that I find remarkably hopeful. This book offers a set of principles showing how a growing number of both corporations and individuals can help lift humanity toward frugality.

My theory may be unwanted news in the eyes of sun-drenched farmers or rural intellectuals, but I am talking here about the clear majority of us—no matter our nation, beliefs, or circumstances.

This is the only higher fact missing from the great old classics that I admire and quote. Not until this century could we even begin to seriously consider city-states as corporate in a global sense. Before the time of kings and lords, we had regional control. Then, we had government in control for a period of many centuries. But much has changed in this new century of the customer and this new time of globalization.

For today, a new higher fact reigns supreme—that cities grow as they enhance the efficiencies of production. The London of Charles Dickens was very different from this. Today the new global city seeks efficiency with grace and force and speed.

This century is about the logic of both capitalism and megacities: the physical manifestation of a new kind of twenty-first-century global capitalism that ceaselessly seeks to improve in a swift and severe way.

Is this all for the good?

Of course, it is not.

But we need to start with the facts, or at least reconcile ourselves to the facts and learn to work together. I now believe Benjamin Franklin was one of the first people on Earth to recognize these higher facts.

The United Nations Millennium Project examined, through nine richly detailed books, how the old forms of industrial capitalism led to more than two dozen failed states—from Somalia to open islands and select Latin states. Nearly 1.5 billion of the world's inhabitants live in areas where poverty is on the rise. It would be naïve to say that capitalism has been kind to these places, but it is blind to stop with that statement.

Corporate globalization is not something new or something that we can plan for or decide upon. Just as physical as our megacities, it is already here. What is lagging is our understanding of the value shift. Virtually no spot on Earth is shielded from the actions of large multinationals. There are few citizens whose days are not directly shaped by the choices of these firms, from the food we make for dinner to the tools we use to get our jobs done and keep our families safe.

The Truth about Global Corporations

According to United Nations studies, almost three-quarters of the world's population will live in cities by 2050, a mere 40 years from now. Oil, energy, personal mobility, and the price of goods are the central variables that have made—and will make—rapid urbanization possible.

Never before in human history have so many lived so densely. The trends projected for 2030 and 2050 make doing more with less a mission critical. The self is now surrounded by the demands of a more efficiently built environment. Each life must prove more efficient.

We already live in a world where, for the first time in human history, most people live in urban megaclusters. Most of your water, air, housing, and food have been processed by corporations before you use them. My premise is simple:

Megacompanies should have mega-responsibilities. This is a fundamental higher fact, like the high-rises in most Islamic states, and the skyscrapers in Manhattan and London and Rome. Think of this intelligent form of competition as the organizational equivalent of the big architectural statements that megacities create, to embody what the human race has become. I always think this thought in a Barcelona or Rome, so why not before a Google or a GE?

We should expect more from these corporations simply because they are in charge of so many aspects of our lives. And of course this takes a new kind of social leader.

Capitalism Today and Tomorrow

I first began thinking about the constraints on carbon, capital, and capitalists in the late 1980s, on a boat ride from Manhattan to Albany sponsored by then-governor Mario Cuomo. The governor and his deputy, Stan Lundine, had organized a 50-person thought experiment called New York 2000. It involved a boat ride up the Hudson, during which the participants would debate the legitimate role of government in securing a better New York, from the city itself to the upstate hinterlands.

Most of the folks on the boat were lawyers, executives, or bankers; I was there as a sort of corporate resource expert, since my first two books (published in the 1980s) had helped reshape federal laws around hazardous waste management.

As we were passing the citadels of West Point, the governor asked us for our working definitions of altruism. After several attempts at defining why people go beyond the call of duty, David Sive, a Park Avenue attorney and cofounder of the Natural Resources Defense Council, told a story I will never forget. He had been stationed in the Italian Alps during World War II. Guarding a snowy summit, he was under orders to shoot anyone who came across the valley and didn't know the Allied Forces' code word, which changed nightly.

A figure approached in the early morning, barely visible in the blinding whiteout. Reciting his orders to himself, Dave thought, "Shoot, you fool." But he didn't shoot. He ignored the orders of his superiors. He decided to resist tradition and his own past practice. The figure turned out to be an Allied soldier who was lost—and therefore didn't know the password either.

Dave finished the story by asking, "And you suppose I didn't shoot for some altruistic reason?" He paused so his audience could weigh in. Most people felt he was a hero. He did not.

It wasn't altruism that stopped him. "My loaded gun remained loaded that morning not due to any higher selfless good," he explained. "Yes, I saved that nameless Allied soldier from death, not because I knew he was on our side, nor because I somehow sensed he had been lost in the storm for three days."

The pause was palpable. "I did it out of basic fear. I was afraid I would make a mistake." The candor of his confession has consequences. Great humans are accepting because they fear making a mistake. Thus, let's celebrate and refocus on the incredible diversity of people, monies, and languages in the great megacities.

Capitalism is at a crossroads, as Stuart Hart likes to phrase it, because a growing number of people who head and support businesses have within them the desire to help make a better world, even if it means they need to kill prior inherited prejudices. These are the captains of tomorrow, the navigators of today's megacities, the inward pioneers to frugality.

One of the best ways to eliminate prejudice and destructive practices is to cut through waste with frugality. This cultural openness is the newest element in advanced capitalism. Thomas Jefferson and Benjamin Franklin were right: we achieve the likelihood of peace through commerce, through the efficient encounter of values with others. I have found that our megacities are full of innovative and peace-loving everyday heroes like those described later.

Although these leaders are fiercely competitive, their biographies show them to be peace loving and diplomatic change agents. In general, they hold their fire, allowing diversity to fill their streets and populate their megacities.

From Benjamin Franklin to Martin Luther King Jr., history shows that it is entirely possible to realign money, people, and rules. We can best do this by asking an audience to do more with less in a visual, personal, valid, and passionate manner. The hidden hand of open and fair competition helps that same audience understand the historic circumstances of the choices before them.

These folks just knew all this early, before billions were born. If you go back over these exceptional lives, you'll see abundant examples of how Jacques Cousteau, Bob Stiller, Martin Luther King Jr., and Alexander Graham Bell each learned how to compete for more with less.

I have met four of these leaders, so please keep in mind that I am writing from direct experience.

Bob Stiller, of Green Mountain Coffee Roasters (GMCR), is almost legendary in his ability to foster a work environment where people embrace fun and loyalty, and growth is propelled by social, not just financial, capital. I met him when I asked him to speak to 80 of our global clients in Phoenix. His firm's stock has risen faster than Starbucks in the last four years (a $7,100 bet 60 months ago in GMCR is now worth $244,000).

Such examples of noticeable yield in the quality of the work experience, matched by exceptional financial returns, explain why social response capitalism is becoming fashionable in the bigger cities and beginning to challenge the luxury and excess that shaped spending patterns in the cities of yesterday.

Some lives, such as those lived by Franklin and Edison, have always been frugal. I met Jacques Cousteau after he signaled that he had read my 1980s books on hazardous waste. When we met, often with his chief scientist near, I could see that he embodied classic principles of frugality in the manner in which he did everything under the sea. In a way, undersea adventure is an exercise in doing more with less oxygen, less equipment, and more visual immediacy. The adventurers on the *Calypso* did much with little. The same goes for the new-century leaders you will meet in your day.

The Crossroads to Motivated Thinking

Although I do not believe I can claim that a total shift has occurred in my last 40 years, I do see a great divide in my travels, and that divide is making winners of the frugal. I see the wasteful, the profligate, the indulgent, and the prejudiced losing more than they are gaining.

The question, again, boils down to the choices we make as we go urban.

We all know that people with convictions are hard to change. If you simply tell them you disagree, they will turn away and ignore you. If you appeal to pure logic, they say you fail to see the evidence or accuse you of thinking too highly of yourself. In my mind, the logic of entrenched thinking has shortened the inventiveness and creativity of far too many lives.

We end this chapter on cities with a reflection on how megacities can help us achieve this next more open, more frugal, golden age.

There is a better way to think through our predicaments, and I think it involves a new science-based way of thinking about predicaments. The theory of motivated reasoning builds from a key insight of modern neuroscience. Here, in a nutshell, is what the neuroscientists, who are taking some baby steps toward human-choice theories, are beginning to note.

Reasoning is always suffused with emotion—what scientists call *affect*. The literary greats and the leaders of people have always known this, but now it can be measured on mental maps. Not only are reason and emotion deeply inseparable, but our inherited or dominant patterns of thinking about money, people, and rules are deeply rooted in us by the time we pass our teen years. I noted this in the earlier chapter, when reflecting on what I knew by age 10.

And further education, or professionalization, only deepens one's belief system, according to these researchers. So our brains are wired to reject threatening new information about a world with 7 billion souls. We must take this as a given, before we begin to talk about it in a more sensible and lasting way.

There are many good reasons for this recalcitrant aspect of the self. Some write entire books about how we make decisions in the blink of an eye. In many ways, David Sive's story contains elements of that kind of blink. This ability to make quick decisions should not be surprising, as we evolved in a fashion that required our slow, erect bodies to react very quickly to threats in our environment, without the eyesight of a hawk or the speed of a cougar.

Thus, a kind of prejudice in the face of higher facts is a basic human survival skill. We push the threatening away.

We pull the friendly closer. We prejudge in the moment. We apply our fight-or-flight reflexes with ease and grace and force, refusing to entertain the new and threatening for too long. We awake each morning with our expectations, forgetting the ugly or unwanted details or events that might have occurred the prior day. In other words, we are not fully or consciously reasoning at all, in the formal sense.

We often think in our ordinary lives that we are scientists, but we actually act like lawyers, reasoning to a preferred or predicted end. But as we approach the near future and densely urbanized settings, social scientists notice things change. We are more open to learn the lessons of competitive frugality when we look at it in terms of decades, not days. The same goes for political compromises on budget crises and budget concessions.

This is why I am writing this book about change management in the common terms of social history, not neuroscience. I believe that adopting the spirit of frugality in full is not very likely, or fully necessary, in my life. Still, I believe we all must remain adept in the short run, to its demands, and adaptive in the long run.

We still have some time to make profound mistakes. This is something the entire advocacy movement neglects. What this means to me—and perhaps to you, as you navigate your next jobs and the fate of your family—is that we must accept that we all wear blinders and use informed preference in most circumstances. We see what we expect to see. Yet there is room enough to grow, if only you adopt the principles of frugality.

So Human an Animal

So we must end this book with the next order of questions: What can we do in the face of human nature?

Given the force of our inherited beliefs about superabundance, entitlement, destiny on Earth, one item is becoming manifestly clear: If I want you to accept new evidence about a world shaped by 7 billion people, I must make my case in a context that doesn't immediately threaten a defensive emotional and blocking reaction from page 1. In other words, we need to remain competitive, remain essentially all too human, without descending into unsustainable greed. Change in human societies is only possible in this step-by-step fashion, if we are to pursue this new golden age without excessive bloodshed.

So now let's add our awareness of megacities and the individual's role in determining his or her own life arc to the major economic shifts available in the next few years, so you can leave this reflection with a snapshot of things to come. There is nothing more significant than to note how globalization has divided our world into various economic speed sets: the mature markets, for example, of Europe and North America, and the faster speeds felt in the Asian tiger nations, Brazil, and China. Figure 5.4 illustrates why emerging economies will soon have the cash flow necessary to compete in new, truly innovative ways.

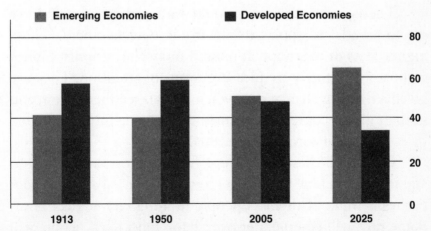

FIGURE 5.4 Percentage Share of Gross Domestic Product (GDP)
Note: At purchasing-power parity.

The fundamentals of this chart have consequences. Rising wealth in emerging economies such as Brazil and China will lead to more competition, which will be, again, first felt in the great megacities. Due to the speed of global information systems, this will rapidly lead to a new golden era where the arts of competitive frugality will reign supreme.

We have traveled far since the beginning of this book.

I hope you now see the design. This book's architectonics are visible. I did not want this book to be repetitive, as much an incantatory, drawing you from related room to room. There is a complex relationship between the self and society that competitive frugality allows, and it unfolds over time into positions of immense inventiveness and social diplomacy. We cannot hold these links to be self-evident, to each reader, region by region of this world, so we develop them chapter by chapter, incantation by incantation.

This is the only way to give higher facts in a world dominated by a vast universe of consumer goods. And it is the only way to build an argument in the face of motivated reasoning.

There is so much we would rather think about, from sex to scandal to sports to electronic entertainment. These higher facts of overpopulation and mounting scarcity cannot compete with the more pleasing forms of attention. They are given a fighting chance only when we can see them anew, and in their global context, in a world that is by nature dominated by regional and parochial interests.

Perhaps the best thing I took from my years as a professor and lobbyist is how to work a crowd of angered and different parties. I think of them as people in a big city at rush hour: Some rage will emerge, but overall, on most days, people will seek the efficient escape route. We are, after all, sharing the same sun, the same boat oars, if you will, and sharing the same limited time on Earth.

Going Back to the School of Social Leadership

Certainly, the city of the future needs the engines of capitalism: cars, computers, better manufacturing, everything that Karl Marx recognized as "the means of production." Social response capitalists are bringing these means to common ends, and our megacities are filled with the results.

So in the end, what makes a megacity an accurate mirror of what capitalism has become? The word *social* has been melded to the word *capital* by these reported developments in a way that would have seemed unthinkable a mere 50 years ago. And herein lie the secrets of outpacing the emotional response that defeats the needed changes. I believe that this very important historical development boils down to a new way of understanding value, both the value in one's firm and the value of one's role as an economic instrument shaping a responsible society.

Megacities make all of us sense a larger purpose and our role in it. By their very nature, they inspire us to dream big and suggest that we can become more. They are the beehives in which we see our honey; they give us our direction and our sense of what we must protect.

Coda

I will make you a bet, one which cannot and will not be collected in my lifetime: that the businesses that survive this challenging new millennium will be the ones that find new and lasting ways to answer key social questions about poverty, mobility, and energy diversity *now*, before all the great megacities do.

And those who answer best will be the makers of the great cities. Golden ages are times of peace, creativity, prosperity, and openness all at once. If you dislodge one, you hurt another, as defilement is never an isolated event.

Today, Tomorrow, Megacities

Fewer than 100 years ago (less than twice my age ago), most centers of capitalism were nation-based hubs of commercial and political capital. They were defined by national goals and national interests, such as those of England or America or Australia.

After having read this chapter, you can see how far we've migrated from the model of the Cold War between the United States and the Soviet Union. We can, and must, become like Benjamin Franklin all over again. So what does this tell me about you, and about the future of your firms?

I wrote this chapter simply to observe how capitalism and megacities have coevolved since World War II, much like a hand growing to its limits in a glove or a pair of sisters learning to transcend rivalry as they age. When you watch these amazing instances of human growth, you have faith we can defeat prejudice and grow through the arts of competitive frugality.

In short, whether you are in London, Istanbul, or Beijing, you cannot compete for real visceral sustainable growth nowadays without thinking through the developments outlined here. The only way to sustain a life and a family and a path forward in this swift and severe world is clear. I admit there will be variances, but really only one collective way.

Sure, some cities will grow like arms dealers through short-term greed, but they will not last long. My bet involves human cultural history, not individual greed and individual denial. The next golden age is near, as evident in our great cities.

Summary in Terms of Social Response Capitalism

Capital, commerce, big cities, and the fate of our climate have coevolved. Since World War II, they have grown sensibly interdependent, high above the faltering policies and financial schemes now before us. People, money, and rules align best around product choices that are supportable, rather than just around rules and regulations. People use money to buy their near future.

What matters most is the sheer adventure of all of this. Capitalism and the city have evolved like sisters, not enemies. They spend a lot of time planning and talking, questioning each other, and regulating behaviors. But in the end, the family of capitalism leads to the kinds of globalized megacities I've visited on my travels.

Whether you are growing up in the newly emerging cities of Brazil, China, or India, or maturing an approach in cities in the old world of Europe and North America, this chapter brings you home in our globalized but still not flat world. The new key is to strike the appropriate balance between competitiveness and frugality in all of us.

I see this instinctive art of competitive frugality ascending our globe. I sense it forming a tidal wave and moving across the globe. It will change and revitalize the Anglo-American way by 2020, and it is already changing many areas of the world overnight.

Of course, there will be pockets of industrial and public resistance to this call for competitive frugality. There will be years of political doubt, voiced by talking heads who are mostly accountants and legal experts. And there will be long procedural delays, while the best firms laugh their ways to the bank on frugality. There will be periods that historians will describe as eras of rampant regional indulgence by consumers in pursuit of a fading happiness.

But overall, the redemptive force we find is a force as primal as human and natural history.

What I write about is international and as large as continuous waves at high tide. Some megacities will recognize the new realities faster than others and find the new balance—and, unfortunately, some cities (and firms) will not.

I have witnessed in my consulting work, without a doubt, a massive change in the mind-set of the leaders of MNCs. In my 30-year memory, this sea change is mostly new. When I wrote my 1990 Simon & Schuster book *In Search of Environmental Excellence*, for example, a mere 20 years ago, there was hardly a ripple of change for sustainability and environmental excellence. Today, many of you are ready to answer the call for a new generation of management tools, new principles for life, and more efficient designs that allow us to go global as we go greener.

How could this happen, if humans are so reluctant to change? The answer is physical and historical, not just emotional and person-based. Individuals may change slowly, but society's beehive jives and jumps. From this view, we change like Edmund Wilson's ant colonies: in groups and in sequence, almost beyond the perception of individuals.

New Grounds for Hope

I see many of you ready to meet the needs of our changing cities and climate, despite political confusion or serious corporate foot-dragging. You seem ready to build net-zero-energy buildings and ready to create the levees needed to answer rising sea levels in Venice, in New Orleans, and in Washington's precious military corridors. I see many in the technical realm ready to construct large-scale mass transit systems for modern mobility. These are the new grounds to spread frugality with our support and protect a civilization.

It is clear that this new kind of capitalism is exactly what is needed in our world's megacities.

The tide may shift rapidly to danger and stark darkness unless we become frugal in time. I see it as a 20- to 30-year window of great opportunities for all. What I've observed about the relationship between capital and cities is likely to be at the center of a series of serious public choices about doing more with less for decades to come.

There is not enough fencing and cement in the world to wall you off from the rest. There is a strong, frontal rudeness to some of these physical facts, like death itself. It is up to you to either accept this future or be isolated by it.

★ Cities such as Athens, Istanbul, Paris, New York, London, and Sydney are the result of competition for greater efficiency. They are going green as they go global.

★ The most efficiently run cities are like the best corporations, resisting the urge to grow blindly. They consider the greater effects of their design.

★ Corporations and their fearless leaders have the ability to impact the near future more significantly by being frugal today.

★ Firms such as Green Mountain Coffee Roasters are challenging the luxury and excess that have shaped spending patterns in today's cities.

★ Change will occur from corporations' response to social problems such as poverty, mobility, and energy diversity, and cities will follow their lead into the near future.

An Idler in the City: Capitalism Is Where We Live
Summary

CHAPTER

6

Another Day Will Tell

Thus the old gentleman ended his harangue. The people heard it, and approved the doctrine, and immediately practiced the contrary, just as if it had been a common sermon; for the auction opened, and they began to buy extravagantly. . . . However, I resolved to be the better for the echo of it; and though I had at first determined to buy stuff for a new coat, I went away, resolved to wear my old one a little longer. Reader, if thou wilt do the same, thy profit will be as great as mine. I am, as ever, thine to serve thee.

—Benjamin Franklin, *The Way to Wealth*

Franklin's warnings are special, like the clever caution here. Seldom predictable, always insightful and resourceful, Franklin reaches across 300 years to you.

How does he do this? Yes, keep your old coat on, my friends, he suggests, for it is better to keep than to waste. Be prepared for many to ignore the warnings before us, but view that as a competitive advantage to you. This could make some of our shared future quite chilling, while it offers you a new way to wealth.

I consider Franklin to be a friend for several reasons. While so many squander value, he compounded it for me. And although I normally like my friends alive, his sharp attacks on waste, the ways he outmaneuvered the average knuckleheads during his life, and his smart pleas for us to be industrious and frugal resonate in me like a Beethoven symphony. His way of speaking is about shaping our way in the near future, about sailing into new frontiers boldly and with positive effect. He informed, persuaded, and delighted, rather than simply informed.

Franklin's sportive seriousness sounds like music to our ears, even after centuries. He is clever. He is honest. He is open. He knew that people will be people, girls will be girls, boys will be boys, yet he embraced changing rules with grace and wit as he matured. And he always remembered, in a primal way, that money will shine its horrible truths onto people; his observations about money, people, and rules remain strong and steady, however much history changes.

There will be winners and losers, but with time, more winners than losers overall. Some will be swamped by fate, while others will be lifted by it. Franklin's words have a higher fidelity to them, like a serious jingle. They sound right even before you reason through them. But where will the new songs of this century come from?

The Element of Surprise

The third and last principle that I discuss is the umbrella concept that you have encountered in this book. It might help you write your own song of competitive frugality. The refrain is "doing more with less is success." We call this the umbrella concept because it helps you come in from the rain of the modern world and live that life of self-determination you crave.

Doing More
with Less

Risk Management

Social Trends

Satisfying Customers

Innovation

Eliminating
Waste/
Reducing Cost

FIGURE 6.1   The Umbrella Concept

You can now add the skills from Figure 6.1 to your days on earth. After some thought, perhaps we can add other key phrases such as "squaring your powers with social needs," "self-determination based on restraint," "aligning money, people, and rules for a smaller world," and "finding surprising and innovative solutions." Here you begin to sense the ultimate domain of this book. I am not writing so much about a new age, as a return to a sense of the self in society that goes way back, and yet is ready—with force and grace—for tomorrow.

In each part of this book, you have reflected in deeper and deeper ways on this mantra or set of meanings, from watching it in sports and competition to examining new forms of policy in health care and environmental protection based on competing on frugality.

This repetition through returning and circling back, was, of course, deliberate. Those who play musical instruments know that composers put false cadences in their work to help listeners refocus their attention. I have found that gifted conversationalists and executives do this as well—almost instinctively—as do superb public speakers. No one can make it past 90 minutes without being rekindled this way. It is the same with six-chapter books.

I respect deeply your patience to have made it this far in this adventure.

Coming Home with Ben Franklin

The best citizens achieve results in their lives this way. They know the ends and the means, and they frugally, and competitively, pursue the goal. They remain fully grounded in this adventure. They become neither astral nor idle in their hopes. Doing more with less will bring success. By declaring this end point earlier in your life, by working the principles as a great lawyer works a jury, through guided discovery, you save and excel and succeed through a kind of self-determination rewarded by this global market.

Whether you know it or not, you have arrived in a place of unexpected advantage in feeling the impact of this mantra. You have arrived at the nexus where competition and frugality meet. Here you find the same fundamental set of basic human resources that allows deeper satisfaction in this world. Are you close enough to feel this in your bones and muscles, not just in your head? This is not idealism. It is arrival in this century.

Some call this state of self-determination and creative frugality mindfulness. Many cultures have long traditions of returning the human to this state of mindfulness via meditative calm. We've designed this book as an umbrella to help you come in from the usual rains of modern life and to return, in a sense, to your more established and long-standing sanctuary. Look around, now that you've arrived home. How much more you can do with less.

It may prove the same with you. The arrival is yours; this book is here simply to guide you, to help you discern how to remain in the game for the future, without losing your footing in humanity. And that has as much to do with you and your friends as with me and my principles.

I believe you need to load these new songs of competitive frugality onto your iPod, take it to the gym, and let the songs play as you work out. You need to wire them into your family, wherever they gather for feasts and festivities. What you once called your time for yoga, your time for reading, your time for self-discovery, might soon become your entire day.

Cultural creatives often achieve this wholeness in their lives. They come to a point where work is life and life is playful discovery, and they often achieve that freedom from fate through frugality and friendship, not through excess or constant doing. Watch Allison Krauss, for example, as she masters her duets with James Taylor or John Waite. She is concise, friendly, loyal, and appreciative—all the principles we have laid out in this book about innovation and scarcity. There is a musicality to the thrust behind this book.

As a social historian, I hope you end this read with a sense of where the world is headed, and with some of the pleasures and profits and friends derived from catching the drift early, so as not to be blindsided by its swiftness and severity. This world waits for no one, my friends.

A Final Hint

Here is a final hint on your way. There are stresses now in your life. In response, I hope to provide, in closing, access to a lovely song, and with it, suggestions on how to reduce the stress.

James Taylor and Mark Knopfler sing a delicious historical ballad called "Sailing to Philadelphia." I have listened to this duet about the creators of the Mason-Dixon Line with wide-eyed appreciation, amazed at how the songwriter suggests so much in so little space. It lifts me, even when I am depressed or discouraged.

The song is rich with historical narrative, as the two explorers, Charles Mason and Jeremiah Dixon, are both in the wild and very much in their heads. They are so different in their own ways, yet they share a risky mission to "chart the Indian sky." They know that they are making a new America, and they know that this new world awaits their decisions. They are taking required risks, realigning money, people, and rules by the line they draw for their time—the Mason-Dixon Line.

The feeling in the song is not so much about undaunted or macho courage, even though the words Taylor sings suggest that the men know that their work may prove fatal. Instead, the song celebrates the well-traveled journey and a life that is worth living, as one encounters both freedom and fate.

Mason and Dixon can feel the weight of an opponent's warring difference nearing them. The listener can also feel the weight of Indians near. As the surveyors turn into a new bay, they look beyond the current horizon of worry, beyond the bay, to where "Another day will make it clear./Why your stars should guide us here."

There is a very human feeling in this song, this willingness to do what you must, knowing resistance, but knowing another day will tell all.

In any work of consequence—from child rearing to building a company—the next days are the ones that matter.

As Franklin often noted, you dig yourself out of a constrained past each day and become better tomorrow.

The only way to transcend the foreboding that surrounds us, the only way to outsmart the logic of limits in our lives, is to rediscover that primary frugality at our start. Mason and Dixon brought this with them to the frontier, and James Taylor brings the same in his voice. If there were a human gene for it, we should have it cloned.

Many of the principles in this short book, such as the statements about the art of competitive frugality, will become more real over time. As we turn the corners into our shared tomorrows, these principles will unfold with more force and certainty. Can you feel that now?

In this book I celebrate some of the early adopters of these principles, from Marcus Aurelius to Benjamin Franklin to E. F. Schumacher. But they only began what you can finish in your life. They saw the need to compete for frugality, sustainability, and new products, long before the advent of wall-to-wall people and stricter environmental and financial rules.

They sailed into their near future as avid adventurers. But what matters most is the tidal flow now forming. The fundamentals of money, people, and rules, although constantly subject to politics and the whims of fate, have some lasting fixed features. They fit us like Franklin's old coat, which he wisely chose to keep.

The future importance of competition and frugality will mount with time. When, for example, the 7 billionth human is born into this world, or the 8 billionth, or the 10 billionth, the equations of this book will take on a starker kind of truth. Life for each of us is short, and anguish abounds. Having written this book, what I know is that you can feel and discover and control your future through frugality.

Each person adds a further reason to compete for frugality. I cannot erase the anguish evident in the needs of people on our Earth, nor can I obliterate the pain of poverty, the shantytowns, the bribed officials, or the weak leaders of my daughter's near future. But there is another way to this future. It is yours, or it is not. That is the choice before you.

Writers write to transform their physical bodies into word bodies. But the physics surrounding their short lives remain immutable. These rules of humanity are set, as when Mason and Dixon saw through their warring opponents to an eventual Philadelphia.

The principles and physics for frugality are set now before us. The chance to repress their importance is weakening with each new birth.

As the individual mantra in Figure 6.2 demonstrates, we cannot change the physical facts, but we can and must change ourselves, as we make, grow, and live.

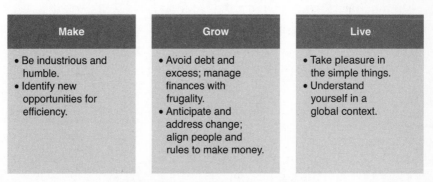

Make	Grow	Live
• Be industrious and humble. • Identify new opportunities for efficiency.	• Avoid debt and excess; manage finances with frugality. • Anticipate and address change; align people and rules to make money.	• Take pleasure in the simple things. • Understand yourself in a global context.

FIGURE 6.2   An Individual Mantra

About the Author

Bruce Piasecki has written eight books over 30 years. Since 1981, he and his senior associates have worked for hundreds of companies through his management advisory firm, the AHC Group (www.AHCGroup.com).

You may wish to visit www.DoingMoreWithLessBook.com for podcasts and new media on this book and Piasecki's firm.

Also by Bruce Piasecki

The Surprising Solution: Creating Possibility in a Swift and Severe World (Sourcebooks, 2010).

World Inc. (Sourcebooks, 2007).

Environmental Management & Business Strategy: Leadership Skills for the 21st Century (John Wiley & Sons, 1998).

Corporate Environmental Strategy: The Avalanche of Change Since Bhopal (John Wiley & Sons, 1995).

In Search of Environmental Excellence: Moving Beyond Blame (Simon & Schuster, 1990).

America's Future in Toxic Waste Management: Lessons from Europe (Quorum Books, 1987).

Beyond Dumping: New Strategies for Controlling Toxic Contamination (Quorum Books, 1984).

Corporate Strategy Today (CST). A monograph series published by the AHC Group, Inc. Titles include:

Leading Corporate Strategies and Climate Change: A Few Key Business Examples (AHC Group, 2006).

The Path to Growth: Building Corporate Value Through Social Leadership (AHC Group, 2005).

Corporate Environmental Strategy: The Journal of Environmental Leadership. Founding Editor, issues 1–46.

Index

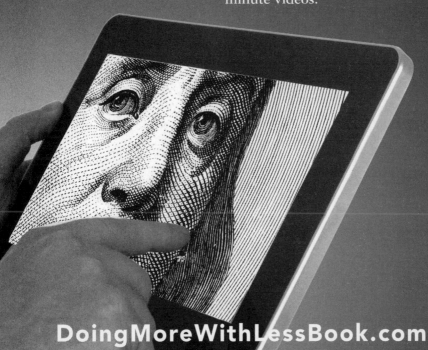

AHC Group, Inc.
Since 1981

Near Future Training for Global Citizenship

There are a set of core competencies that the next generation of business managers need to be in command of.

The AHC Group is uniquely positioned to help promising leaders from your firm learn the essential skills needed to manage at the highest level. If you believe that existing internal mentoring and training programs address these issues to some extent, but more focused development could be helpful, please contact us today.

The AHC Group Senior Associates each have years of experience at major companies as leaders of their EHS and Sustainability programs. The real world experience of these senior associates includes development and delivery of corporatewide and global training programs on policies and specific technical subjects, managing and facilitating internal benchmarking sessions, focused process improvement workshops, and individual mentoring for high potential employees.

Change Management and Training Future Leaders

1. Do you have tomorrow's leaders ready to lead your company into the future?
2. What if you needed to be replaced tomorrow? Is your replacement ready?
3. Have you prepared your replacement so he or she can build on your legacy?
4. Succession planning is your responsibility. How would you grade yourself?
5. Consider the skills you have developed—have you done what is needed to develop your replacement's skills?

AHC Group, Inc.
Since 1981

Near Future Training for Global Citizenship

Senior EHS and Sustainability Executives often do not have the time needed to effectively train and develop their future leaders. The AHC Group can help to provide some of this needed mentoring in a way that allows for successful succession of executive corporate leadership, while simultaneously helping your company maximize business value from sustainability and position itself for the near future.

AHC Group Customizable Offerings in Leadership Training

- AHC hired on retainer for 1–2 or more years as a leadership advisor for individuals or small groups within your company.

- Regularly scheduled discussions with the trainee on specific topics critical to the enterprise and to the trainees' unique strengths and areas for growth.

- On call to serve as a mentor, advisor, confidant when discussing specific issues that the trainee encounters on the job, and to discuss options for how to successfully manage these issues.

- Trainee's exposure to external experts in handling issues that are particularly critical to the trainees' professional growth. This exposure could be in private settings or as part of more public meetings, conferences, workshops, classes.

- Recommendations about books or seminars that advance the trainee's development, with follow-up discussions.

- Benchmarking with executives in similar roles from different companies.

AHC Group • 156 Stone Church Road • Ballston Spa, New York 12020 • 518.583.9615 • www.AHCGroup.com

AHC Group, Inc.
Since 1981

Near Future Training for Global Citizenship

Traits Needed for Successful Sustainability Leadership

1. Understanding the broad context
2. Managing complexity, coping with uncertainty
3. Systems thinking
4. Working beyond boundaries
5. Leading change
6. Enabling innovation

 World Business Council for Sustainable Development

Since 1981 the AHC Group, a general management consulting firm headquartered in Saratoga Springs, New York, has specialized in the critical areas of corporate governance consultings, energy and environmental strategy, product innovation, and sustainability strategy.

Through our consulting contracts, business leadership seminars, and strategy and growth publications, we have helped hundreds of companies to realize the business potential in environmental and public issues, enhance stakeholder and investor relations, and position themselves better in the marketplace.

AHC Group • 156 Stone Church Road • Ballston Spa, New York 12020 • 518.583.9615 • www.AHCGroup.com